Jesus Power

Sherwood Eliot Wirt

Jesus Power

Harper & Row, Publishers

New York
Evanston
San Francisco
London

To Eugenia
daughter in love

Grateful acknowledgment is made for permission to quote from the following: four lines from "A Prayer (Be Thou My Vision)," in *The Poem Book of the Gael*, selected and edited by Eleanor Hull, courtesy of the estate of Eleanor Hull and Chatto & Windus Ltd. (London); excerpts by Wang Ming-tao in *Come Wind, Come Weather* by Leslie T. Lyall, © 1960 by Moody Press, Moody Bible Institute of Chicago; lines from *Look Homeward, Angel* by Thomas Wolfe, © 1957 by Edward C. Aswell, Charles Scribner's Sons (New York) and William Heinemann, Ltd. (London); lines from *The Unutterable Beauty* by G. A. Studdert-Kennedy, and *The Effective Evangelist* by Lionel B. Fletcher, by permission of Hodder & Stoughton Ltd. (London); two lines of "The Hollow Men" by T. S. Eliot, in *Collected Poems 1909-1962*, published by Harcourt Brace Jovanovich, Inc. (New York) and Faber & Faber Ltd. (London).

FIRST EDITION

STANDARD BOOK NUMBER: 06-069603-6

LIBRARY OF CONGRESS CATALOG CARD NUMBER: 72-78059

Contents

Foreword

by Billy Graham

IN my travels on different continents I have been thrilled to visit churches that glowed with a warmth I found hard to explain in ordinary terms. The pulpits rang with the sound of the Gospel, and pews were filled with worshipers. I also found churches in which the light had faded and the warmth had died away. The ministers were confused and their messages were punctuated with doubt and uncertainty. The congregations seemed to be living on a heritage of the past—the faith of their ancestors—while the world was passing them by.

The difference, I believe, was the presence and power of the Holy Spirit of God. That is why I welcome this new book by a member of our team, Sherwood Wirt. Dr. Wirt is concerned about the question of spiritual power in the church. He believes that men and women come to church looking for this power, and when they don't find it, they look elsewhere. He also believes that the Bible teaches a worldwide revival is possible before the return of our Lord Jesus Christ, and that the hour of that revival may be upon us.

I am happy to commend his inquiry to the reading public. I agree that many evidences of revival are present, and that ours is a thrilling moment in which to proclaim the Gospel. Dr. Wirt holds a doctor of philosophy degree from Edinburgh University, and is a minister of the United Presbyterian Church. For the past twelve years he has been a working journalist serving as editor of *Decision* magazine. This position has afforded him, I believe, an unusual opportunity to view the life of the church in the world today. He has made a thoughtful examination of supernatural power both in Scripture and in contemporary Christian living. I pray this volume will lead many to understand, to appropriate, and to put to use those characteristics of the Gospel of Jesus Christ that have always marked the ministry of a vigorous and effective church.

Preface

FOR two thousand years the Gospel of Jesus Christ has shown remarkable survival value while one religion after another has coughed, sputtered, and died. Obviously the Gospel has "something going for it," but what is that something? The New Testament says it is Jesus Christ himself. Those of us who accept Biblical truth claim that nothing in the universe or beyond it can compare with the power of the living Christ. But when we speak of Christ's power exactly what do we mean? Tó examine the word "power" in the context of faith is the purpose of this book.

Writing it has been one of the most exhilarating experiences of my life. It has been like peeking through a keyhole of God's creation and watching what makes it work. I have sat at the sandals of some of history's most wonderful people, and have dipped my Dixie cup into the sacred fountain of truth. Time and again my spirit has been lifted by an unseen force as outside events have confirmed that God is present today in saving power.

While sitting in the press box at the Oakland, California Coliseum during an evangelistic crusade in the summer of 1971, I watched a young man wearing a sweat shirt as he stepped onto the infield to make a commitment to Christ. Painted on the back of his shirt were the words JESUS POWER. I thought, That will be the title of my book. Shortly afterward one of God's quiet miracles took place in our family and we were given a chance to observe the impact of spiritual power at close range.

During the time of this writing, between August, 1971 and February, 1972 the tempo of a revival spirit picked up noticeably in North America. Spiritual awakening was reported in many areas, including Wilmore, Kentucky, where the Asbury College revival of February

1970 continued to be felt; the Pacific Coast, where the Jesus People Movement was growing; and Texas, Illinois, Ohio, Minnesota, North Carolina, and New Mexico, where church revivals were reported. It was a most opportune time to be writing about spiritual power.

Then in the midst of the other evidences, an astonishing visitation of God occurred in some churches in western Canada. By the time these pages had to go to press it was spreading eastward and southward, without publicity and without human organization, under the leading of the Holy Spirit. I have described my encounter with the Canadian revival in Chapter 13.[1] It is my hope that some of the overflowing cup I received in the winter of 1971–72 has spilled onto the pages of this book.

In 1968 I published an examination of the Christian's social conscience, which earnestly attempted to relate the Gospel of Jesus Christ to the issues and concerns of our common life.[2] In a sense the present work is a companion volume to *The Social Conscience of the Evangelical.* The earlier book charted the exterior of the Christian life; this one explores the interior.

While I have concentrated on the supernatural resources of faith, I have tried not to dodge present-day realities or to obscure the agony of the church. We have to recognize the effort being made in Western countries to strip all, or virtually all, supernatural elements from the Christian message. In some theological schools the Bible has been "demythologized." The practice of prayer has been given up. Many agree that "politics is the area in which to seek the will of God today."[3] The tragedy of this realignment is not the taking of the Gospel into the world; that is where it belongs. Nor is it simply disagreement over the Bible; men have always disagreed. The tragedy is that so-called Christian people in places of influence *have forgotten completely about the Holy Spirit.* Such spiritual amnesia cuts off the church's power supply and forces abandonment of the evangelistic task. The shrinking statistics of most denominations in Europe and America fill out the story.

The late Professor Hendrik Kraemer once observed that no matter how desperate the predicament of the church, if Christians will confront it squarely and candidly, something can be done about it.[4] Only when the church refuses to come to grips with reality is its condition beyond remedy. The truth is that God has not changed, and his power is as virile as ever. What Jeremiah said twenty-five hundred years ago still holds today: "Thou hast made the heaven and the earth by thy great power and stretched out arm, and there is nothing too hard for thee."[5] According to the New Testament, that great power is now open to men and ready for use. To halt the secular drift, humanity needs a reaffirmation of the supernatural dimension of existence. Whether or not man has "come of age" (I think today Dietrich Bonhoeffer might question his own statement), he still has a heavenly Father. Relationships between God and man are what they were made at Calvary. Now is still the accepted time, and today the day of salvation.[6]

S.E.W.

Acknowledgments

THIS volume is an expansion of four lectures given in Denver, Colorado in the fall of 1971. The faculty of Conservative Baptist Theological Seminary invited me to deliver the first of its "Christian Thought and Life" series under the sponsorship of the Thomas F. Staley Foundation of New York City. The lectures were entitled "The Power Game," "Jesus Power Defined," "The Great Power Failure," and "Jesus Power Today." I would like to thank the faculty and students of the seminary for their hospitality on that occasion.

To express thanks for the kind of help that goes into such a book as this, I would have to write my spiritual autobiography; yet certain acknowledgments must be made. Dr. Vernon C. Grounds, president of Conservative Baptist Seminary, extended the invitation that sent me to the typewriter. Members of the editorial staff of *Decision* magazine read the chapters and made useful comments. Certain members of the Minnesota Christian Writers' Guild, with whom I shared portions of the book in a study group, gave valuable suggestions. Dr. Harold Lindsell, editor of *Christianity Today,* and Principal Leon Morris of Ridley College, Melbourne, Australia kindly read and corrected the typescript. Dr. Billy Graham graciously contributed the foreword. Mr. George M. Wilson of the Billy Graham Association granted use of material that appeared in the pages of *Decision.* Miss Charlene Anderson arranged for permissions.

My wife Winola and my son Alexander offered some helpful counsel. Finally I would like to thank Miss Kersten Beckstrom, who took charge of the manuscript, improved it at many points, typed it, compiled the notes and index, and saw it through to publication.

S.E.W.

Minneapolis, Minnesota

Chapter 1

The Power Game

> As I began to read the Psalms of David, those hymns of
> faith and devotion that break the pompous spirit, they
> made me literally cry out to you, my God. I was a raw
> beginner, new to your love, and now the Psalms were
> setting me on fire and making me want to shout them to
> the whole world, to counteract the pride of the human
> race.[1]
>
> —AUGUSTINE OF HIPPO (354–430)

COME with me to the entrance of a cave in southern France. It is now
several thousand years before Christ, and from our lookout we are
observing a strange-appearing man as he emerges cautiously into the
sunlight. He is dressed in skins and his hair is long and matted. We
notice that he is carrying something behind his back. It turns out to
be a club.

Now, what does this primitive son of Adam intend to do with that
club? Why does he carry it that way? Is he afraid of sudden attack
by some intruding man or beast? Or is he just going out foraging?

Neither guess is correct. His behavior is not conditioned by fear
or hunger. What is it he wants? He is going after his neighbor. And
why is he looking for his neighbor? He feels that his neighbor is a
threat to his domain, so he has decided to take action that will
eliminate the menace to his hunting preserve and his fishing streams.
But his real interest is not in manslaughter; his aim is to get rid of
the problem. The cave dweller would be willing to make his neighbor into a vassal and slave, if it came to that. As things stand, the

1

neighbor is interfering with environmental control. The point of the club is that once power is established, the interference will end; all will be well; there will be one master and one boss.

To come back to the complexities of our jet age, let us look at some of the descendants of that remote ancestor. We note the influence of heredity, for each one we examine carries a concealed club. Each of them wants power. That's nothing—so do I. So does every man. "Wherever I found a living creature," declared Nietzsche, "there I found the will to power."[2]

Human history is the history of a quest for power. No drive known to the science of behavior can match man's pursuit of personal command. Power plays operate on every level of life, among every variety of peoples, without exception. The man or woman who is helpless and powerless has no real desire to remain that way. Everyone loves power even if he does not know what to do with it.[3] On the other hand, those who have been once intoxicated with power can never willingly abandon it.[4]

Is power more important to man than the satisfaction of his lust or vengeance? Apparently it is. Apparently the key element in all of these drives is the securing of control. With control go status, privilege, authority. Man wants to be on top, and unless checked he will stop at nothing to achieve that end. He does not object to the existence of power as a fact of life; he just wants to make sure he has it. John Locke wrote:

The great question which in all ages has disturbed mankind, and brought on them the greatest part of those mischiefs which have ruined cities, depopulated countries, and disordered the peace of the world, has been not whether there be power in the world, nor whence it came, but who should have it.[5]

What causes man to lunge out on this mad chariot race for personal power? The Bible says it is his vanity, or more accurately, his pride. Thus we read in Ecclesiastes:

I made me great works; I builded me houses; I planted me vineyards; I made me gardens and orchards, and I planted trees in them of all kinds of fruits: I made me pools of water . . . I got me servants and maidens . . . I gathered me also silver and gold . . . I gat me men singers and women singers. . . . So I was great, and increased more than all that were before me in Jerusalem. . . . Then I looked on all the works that my hands had wrought, and on the labor that I had labored to do: and, behold, all was vanity and vexation of spirit. . . .[6]

The early fathers of the church showed great wisdom when they identified original sin as pride rather than lust, greed, or hate. Augustine in particular insisted that pride is the beginning of all sin. "And what is pride," he asks, "but a perverse appetite for the high places? And this lofty ambition becomes perverse when the soul cuts itself off from him who is its Source, and to whom it ought solely to cleave, in order to make the self seem its own source. This happens when the soul is too pleased with itself."[7] All through his *Confessions* runs a refrain which he quotes from 1 Peter: "God resists the proud but gives grace to the humble."[8]

The book of Genesis confirms the view that sin is essentially a power play of human pride. According to the record, the tempter whispered to our first parents, "You will be like God." In what way? In nobility of appearance? In wisdom? In character? But all of these characteristics were already present in Eden. What could they possibly have wanted that they did not have? Note again the word of the serpent in Genesis, "Your eyes will be opened, and you will be like God, knowing good and evil."[9] The answer of the Bible is that man wanted what he has wanted ever since—power. The knowledge Adam sought was the key to power. But power is not evil per se; God already had bestowed upon man a limited exercise of power in Eden. Unfortunately it was not enough, for man wants to rule, to be in charge. So Adam's act of disobedience became a kind of taunt, and Scripture records it as rebellion in the face of Almighty God.

It still is.

We may protest that other living creatures are involved in the power game; they are, but with a difference. When animals struggle for power their behavior is simply a part of the order of nature. The leopard leaps on his prey and drags the carcass to his hideout, but he has not sinned. The fox slips into the chicken coop and slaughters a flock of hens, but he has not sinned.

In contrast is man. He climbs to a seat of power and leaves behind him a trail of broken and bleeding rivals. The blood may not be actual human gore, but it speaks of the wreckage of human lives. The man who did this has sinned. Why has he sinned? Why has he violated the law of God when the animal killers did not? Because, according to the teaching of the Bible, the creatures of the forest did not try to step out of their creaturely roles to assume the authority that belongs to the Creator; the man did.[10] Of course man will try to excuse himself. He will set up his defense and claim that he was driven by insecurity, or fear, or necessity, or an instinct for survival, or the devil, or his animal nature, or by some psychosis over which he had no control. Or, more likely than any of these excuses, he will announce that he was defending himself against an aggressor.

It is not unnatural for a man who is watching a film of a musk ox or a walrus battling its male rivals in the herd and winning control to think to himself, "That's what life is all about. This is a dog-eat-dog world, and I'm going to get the biggest bites." The error lies not in his logic but in his anthropology. He fails to grasp that, while he is a part of the natural order, he is more than that. According to Genesis man is made in the image of God. He is not simply an upward projection of animality; he has a built-in quality of transcendence that our first parents' rebellion did not completely vitiate. Man is a special creation, a spiritual being. Between the lowest form of man and the highest form of animal there is an infinite qualitative difference that can be explained only in spiritual terms. Experimental science does not always recognize this difference, but that does not disprove it; rather such a lapse helps to point up the limitations of science—which many scientists are quick to acknowledge.

Man gives many excuses to justify his reach for power, but they won't stand up. They are at best only secondary motivators. The trait that commands him essentially is his pride. Pride requires power; pride feeds on power; therefore pride sets out to take power. As Reinhold Niebuhr expressed it in his Gifford Lectures:

There is a pride of power in which the human ego assumes its self-sufficiency and self-mastery and imagines itself secure against all vicissitudes. It . . . believes itself to be the author of its own existence, the judge of its own values and the master of its own destiny. . . . Closely related to [this proud pretension] . . . is the lust for power which has pride as its end. The ego does not feel secure and therefore grasps for more power in order to make itself secure [cf. the cave man at the beginning of this chapter]. It does not regard itself as sufficiently significant or respected or feared, and therefore seeks to enhance its position in nature and in society. . . . Man is ignorant and involved in the limitations of a finite mind; but he pretends that he is not limited. . . . All of his intellectual and cultural pursuits, therefore, become infected with the sin of pride. Man's pride and will-to-power disturb the harmony of creation. . . . The religious dimension of sin is man's rebellion against God, his effort to usurp the place of God. The moral and social dimension of sin is injustice.[11]

The injustice of which Niebuhr speaks is injustice inflicted on human beings, for it is on human beings first of all that man in his vanity vents his obsession with power. The cruelest tyrants of history have also been the supreme egoists; but we do not need to exhume the bones of such historic villains as Genghis Khan, Attila, Louis XIV, or Richard III to make the point. In persons of our own era —Hitler, Stalin, and Peron, to name but three—there is plenty of material from which to draw.

To excoriate dictators in words is easy; what is not so easy is to recognize (as Aristotle did long ago) the potential dictator in each one of us. I am not referring to politics; most of us would prefer not to be saddled with the grief of running a nation or a continent. But does that mean we do not wish to be "like God"? Not at all. We just want to be God in our own little corner. Like the cave dweller in southern France, we want to dominate our immediate environment: our home, our block, our club, our business, our department, our town, our circle of friends. That is the only part of the universe that matters to most of us; we say you can have the rest of it. We want the seat of power where we happen to be sitting.

The avenues of attack we employ are as varied as the human imagination can contrive. For example, the late English humorist Stephen Potter offered many ingenious tips to those who wished to use the power game to gain unfair advantage over their fellow men. He developed his approach into a quasi science which he called first "gamesmanship," then "one-upmanship," and finally (and significantly) "lifemanship."[12]

Potter showed the depth of subtlety to which people will descend in the power struggle—something Oliver Goldsmith disclosed two centuries earlier in his comedy *She Stoops to Conquer*. Among the tricks Potter advocated were what he called the "sense of distrust," "glaciation" (deadpan reaction to a joke), "advanced languaging" (by which he meant "to confuse, irritate, and depress by the use of foreign words, fictitious or otherwise"), "religious basic" (Potter's method for making people feel uncomfortable about religion), and the "Canterbury block" (a title he gave to irrelevant interruptions such as "but not in the south").

Potter also developed some secondary techniques which he called "golfmanship," "clothesmanship," "woomanship," and "weekendmanship." His principal doctrine of "lifemanship" he defined as "how to be one-up; how to make the other man feel that something has gone wrong, however slightly." The lifeman he described as "always alert and ready for the slight put-off, the well-timed provocation which will get the other fellow down [and] by ploy or gambit, most naturally gain the advantage." Behind his humor lies the grim truth that the fast ones people like to pull are in fact designed to obtain and maintain power over the other party.

A useful illustration of this principle is found in Eric Berne's best seller *Games People Play*.[13] He describes a game he calls "rapo," which he says "is popular at social gatherings and consists essentially of mild flirtation." A lady signals that she is "available," and then "gets her pleasure from the man's pursuit." But as soon as he has committed himself, the game is over. Why? Because, says Berne, she did not really want sexual contact, or even tactile contact; all she wanted was power over a personality.

What "rapo" tells us is that lust is a form of human pride, so that when a person lusts he is looking beyond physical gratification to domination over another person. The attraction of the sexual element would be sharply reduced without the psychological drive for possession. John seems to imply such a connection in his first letter, though the relationship is not elaborated: "For all that is in the world, the lust of the flesh, and the lust of the eyes, and the pride of life, is not of the Father, but is of the world."[14]

Does man play his power game just with other human beings? Let us take a closer look.

Chapter 2
What Men Want

Spiritual power is the proper longing of God's people.[1]
—CHARLES C. RYRIE

IF the power struggle is a game, it is one that we all play. The sin of human pride is not only "original," it is universal. Power, Lord Acton wrote, tends to corrupt, and absolute power corrupts absolutely.[2] We may object to such a sweeping statement, but if we look at our world honestly we have to acknowledge that virtually everything man undertakes to do he succeeds in corrupting. When two converted Auca Indians from Ecuador, Kimo and Komi, were flown to the Berlin Congress on Evangelism in 1966, they were asked by an interviewer, "What do you think of the white man's civilization?" One of them smiled and said in his dialect, "The white man has all these wonderful things and they are always breaking." Man progresses upward and downward at the same time. He strides toward incredible achievements but the judgment of God is upon each one of them.

The Apostle Paul wrote to the Roman Christians the following evaluation of much of the human race:

They know God, but they do not give him the honor that belongs to him, nor do they thank him. Instead, their thoughts have become complete nonsense and their empty minds are filled with darkness. They say they are wise, but they are fools; instead of worshiping the immortal God, they worship images made to look like mortal man or birds or animals or reptiles. Because men are such fools, God has given them over to do the filthy things

8

their hearts desire . . . to corrupted minds, so that they do the things that they should not.[3]

What Paul is saying is that if men really want to play the power game, God will play it too—but in his own way. He will let our reason become so warped that we end by thwarting our own efforts. So man, intent on power and unaware of who is setting the rules, invents gunpowder to shoot his neighbor but shoots himself. He develops the airplane to bomb his neighbor, but bombs himself.

Social benefits will not content man either. Providing him with more pay, better living quarters, and medical care will not solve his basic problem for the simple reason that he wants more. He wants his neighbor's pay as well as his own; he wants his neighbor's house, and wife too; in short, he wants all he can get—power, domination, glory, and worship from those around him. Power plays are made by children; by men and women of all ages; by cripples; by parents; by corporations; by labor unions; by political blocs; by majority groups and minority groups; by governments; by rich people and poor people; by churches and synagogues; by the armed and the unarmed; and by dead people through their wills.

The Marxists perpetuated the ancient illusion that unregenerate man can be taught to control his power drives. "We must grow men," said Stalin, "as carefully as a gardener grows his plants."[4] But plants and animals do not lie or steal. Marx defined man as a producing animal but never recognized him as a sinner. The result is that Communism was trapped in the same pretensions of pride and the same ideological taint that it recognized in other social systems. The Communist Party secretary is perhaps as power-hungry as the Czar ever was, but (like the Czar) he will not admit his will to dominate because he cannot see it.

The illusion that the quest for power can be humanly controlled goes back at least to Plato, whose otherwise brilliant *Republic* could never take practical form because it was based on erroneous presuppositions about man and power. The same might be said of the utopias designed by dreamers and social idealists over the intervening centuries. Jean Jacques Rousseau proposed a new type of "nature boy" who would give up lusting after power. Auguste Comte projected a technocratic man who would put scientific curbs on his arrogance. Lenin conceived a classless society in which government would "wither away." Curiously, the same utopianism pervades a best seller of the 1970's which is popular among disenchanted youth. Charles A. Reich's *The Greening of America* contains many incisive social observations, but in its final pages we are informed that in the foreseeable future a revolution will bring about "respect for each individual . . . abstention from coercion or violence . . . killing. . . . Respect for the natural environment. . . . Honesty in all personal relations."[5] Evidently Shangri-La is about to appear! But what will happen to man's pride in this coming un-Biblical Paradise? How will his thirst for power be quenched? Who (to quote the old nursery fable) will bell the cat?

Sometimes man's bid for power is bold and naked; sometimes it is concealed in an altruistic and harmless-looking package. The Trojan horse, you will remember, was supposed to be a religious object (a votive offering to Pallas Athene for the Greeks' safe return). Since long before that day deception has played a major role in the struggle for every kind of power, including religious power. Church politics (which may be the most subtle of all forms of political maneuvering) tries to hide the power motive beneath the shibboleths of pious language. Many centuries ago John Chrysostom asked scornfully, "What can be more pitiable than a man who fasts, prays and shows mercy with an eye not only to the glory that comes from above, but to the glory that comes from men?"[6] Even more harmful to mankind than the individual power struggles within a religious establishment has been the collective pride of religion that has caused untold suffering through persecution, bigotry, greed, jealousy, vengefulness, forced conversions, uprooting of populations, and even genocide. There are few people today who would ascribe such activity to anything other than human pride. As William James said, "Religion is a monumental chapter in the history of human egotism."[7]

But pride of religion has provided only one ball park for the power game. There has also been pride of nationality *("Deutschland über Alles"),* pride of race ("they really *are* inferior"), pride of blood ("pure Greek" or "pure Japanese"), pride of language (the posh accent), pride of soil ("our crops have a higher yield"), pride of locale ("girls are prettier here"), pride of skin color ("black is beautiful"), pride of hair color ("gentlemen prefer blondes"), pride of height ("we grow 'em tall"), pride of the shape of one's nose ("mine is aquiline, yours is snub").

All such boasting forms part of man's struggle to dominate his environment. Unless he is convinced that he is really better than others, his will-to-power remains unfulfilled. When the University of Minnesota football team won a trip to the Rose Bowl a few years back, a psychologist reported that the mental health of the entire state had improved because a Minnesota product had come out on top. Minnesotans were vindicated as faster, stronger, more dexterous athletes; thus the state population's instinctive pride was satisfied by a demonstration of power.

Man wishes, however, to conquer other worlds besides the world of human beings. There is the world of nature, the universe around us. Even the concept of a "world" is now obsolete, for man has already reached the earth's one satellite and is now expending tremendous energy to attain other space victories. On his home planet he is literally moving mountains in order to be able to control his environment. Many of his achievements merit the highest praise. He is damming and bridging rivers, desalinating the water of oceans, causing deserts to blossom, working miracles of transportation and communication. He is making vast inroads on his old dread enemy, disease. The age span is being extended; health is being improved; many handicapped persons are now able to lead reasonably normal lives. Basic research is providing man with increasing knowledge of his environment; and as in Eden, knowledge means power.

Ah, but—

Man's drive for domination of nature is creating problems that threaten to destroy him. The ecological crisis has broken over his head. People are aware at last of what they are doing to the good earth, its streams, its lakes, forests, hills, oceans—its very atmosphere. Yet they are making no serious effort to stop. Human indifference is exactly as it was while Noah was building the ark. Spoliation goes on; wildlife species continue to disappear; fish no longer enter the rivers; eagles stop flying; oil slicks ring the beaches; clearcutting denudes the hills; strip-mining turns the valleys into badlands; and the bountiful earth is raped of her mineral resources.

When God gave man dominion over the earth, man was still without sin. In his fallen state, man's quest for power has upset the balance of nature and "disturbed the harmony of creation." Yet such are his anxieties and such is the range of his pride that he refuses to curb his exploitation of natural resources. When the claim has petered out, when the earth has caved in, when the forest is stripped, when the oyster beds are depleted, when the fish come no more to spawn, then he will stop and not before—unless a superior power halts his depredations. Eventually he will discover that he cannot control nature; he can only cooperate with it. By then it may be too late.

The search for power has involved man not only in a struggle to conquer the world of men and the world of nature, but in a far more devious battle to appease and control the supernatural forces in his environment. Since prehistoric times men have known that there is more to the power game than knocking over the opponent with a war club. Homer's *Iliad* is not just the poetic history of a Greek military campaign against Troy; it is an effort to describe through mythology the interplay between man as warrior and the invisible forces that alternately help and thwart his plan of conquest.

The capricious supernatural forces are held to be sometimes divine, sometimes demonic. If man judges them to be good he summons them to his aid; if he judges them bad he tries another tack. He may offer sacrifices to appease them, or invoke the aid of a rival deity to crush them; or he may, as in the legend of Faust, sell his soul for a temporary dispensation of power. Whatever the plan, whatever the device, the aim is the same: to gain a position of strength.

One of the pathetic developments of modern times has been the attempt of youth to achieve a kind of beachhead on the supernatural by experimenting with drugs that "expand" or "blow" the mind. Young people in their teens and twenties today know far more about demonic activity than do their counterparts in the thirties and forties. Whatever the reason given for the drug trip, the real aim is power through freedom from the limitations of the flesh. But it is not simply power over the natural environment that is sought; drug abuse is an attempt to break into a higher power circle, into those shrouded, esoteric regions which superstitious men have always felt had control over circumstances and events. The Pharaoh Rameses had his magicians; King Saul had his witches; Julian the Apostate had his animal entrails; and the modern youth has his occultist paperbacks. In each case knowledge of the supernatural is held to be a means of power —the power man feels he must have if he is to become master of his environment.

"If you will call up the monkey demon," a recently divorced young man was told by a drug pusher in Kentucky, "he will do things for you. He will help you to get even with your enemies. He will cause girls to come and sit on your lap. He will even make you a movie star." And the young man fell into the bear pit, because those were the things he wanted. He then discovered to his terror that he had sold himself to the devil. He was delivered (as he related the story to me), but not until he had called upon a power higher than the occult.[8]

Finally, in his quest for personal power, man has sought to control himself. The human spirit is naturally prone to wander and inherently lazy. The historic church has recognized this tendency as *accidie,* or sloth, also known as sluggishness or torpor. Church tradition has made it one of the seven deadly sins. In spite of it, some men have wanted power badly enough to overcome the drag of inertia. They have put themselves through all manner of physical and mental and even spiritual exercises. Without doubt the stern discipline of the Puritans provided much of the power that discomfited the Royalists. The Jesuits, having subjected themselves to the spiritual exercises of Ignatius Loyola, became the most powerful order in Roman Catholicism.

Men have worn out their eyesight and spent half their lives studying in academic institutions; they have sat, knelt, stood, lain prostrate, swung from ropes; they have fasted and undergone all manner of deprivation and self-inflicted punishment, sometimes in a spirit of pure devotion to God, but more often perhaps to achieve standing and authority among men. Yet it has not proved easy for them to subdue the human mind and spirit, for there are other sins besides sloth. Jerome, the monk, in a worthy moment of honesty, wrote of his futile attempts to bring his body under control while he was living as a hermit in the desert:

> I would sit alone because I was filled with bitterness. My limbs, covered with sackcloth, were an unlovely sight. My face was pale from fasting, and my mind was hot with desire in a body cold as ice. Though my flesh was as good as dead, the fires of passion kept boiling up within me. There I was, self-condemned, with only scorpions and wild beasts as companions; yet I was often surrounded by bevies of dancing girls.[9]

Eventually the man who succeeds in bringing his mental powers and personal life under control is often able (if he so wishes) to move to a position in which he can bring other men under his control. The power motive has suppressed the blandishments of the flesh as few other motives have done. When power has been achieved, the unregenerate flesh reopens its clamor; but in the heat of the struggle for position, strong men have proved able to take command of their own lives.

Yet when they do take command, what then? What is the end result of this atavistic struggle for the "survival of the fittest"? After a man has kicked everyone else off the rungs of the ladder and has scrambled to the top, where is he? And what is his world?

Chapter 3
The Bang or the Whimper

> Whatever creates in me a sense of power tends to make
> me atheistic. How? When I become conscious of the
> possession of any power, I begin to think of myself as a
> cause rather than an effect. I can stir human hearts, I can
> move my fellow men. Recognizing myself as a power, I
> begin to think of myself as a creator, a cause; and ignor-
> ing all the other causes, I lapse into an atheism which
> leaves out God.[1]
>
> —JOHN HENRY JOWETT (1864–1923)

POWER over other people, power over nature, power over supernatural forces, and power over himself. Such is the four-sided goal of
natural man as we see him emerging from a primeval cave with a
club behind his back.

Today he does not live in a cave but in an air-conditioned dwelling, and he is polite to his neighbor because he wants no trouble.
In fact he is tied to a whole host of neighbors by an intricate system
of postal routes, streets, sewers, and telephone and power lines.
Might it not be said that the true picture of man has been distorted
in these pages; that he is not as power-hungry as I have claimed?

Let's look for a moment at the beneficent uses men have made of
power. By banding together in communities they have merged their
individually felt needs into the expression of a common purpose. By
promulgating law codes and hiring legal officers to enforce them
they have made power a vehicle of mutual protection. By introduc-
ing such institutions as the secret ballot and the multiparty system

and by guaranteeing basic judicial rights, they have established the concept of freedom under law.

Mainstream Christianity, according to Vernon C. Grounds, distinguishes between "force" and "violence." Force, says Dr. Grounds, is the power wielded to make and keep human life truly human. Violence he denounces as useless, indiscriminate, and absurd; but he finds that either the threat or the use of force is needed at every level of society to make men behave and obey the rules.[2] The point is important because many Christians are confused about social power. They are puzzled by the seeming lack of interest among New Testament Christians in the proper functioning of a civilized order. Alfred North Whitehead went so far as to say that a generally felt responsibility to maintain society was "almost entirely absent from [New Testament] Christianity."[3] William Ernest Hocking took the same line, claiming that the early Christians renounced the world and "walked the earth as strangers, owing another allegiance, communists, disenchanted. . . ."[4]

If this was the case, why did Jesus bother to heal anyone? Why did he pay his taxes? Why did he condemn fraud and extortion? Why did the disciples appoint deacons to organize the distribution of food in the community? Why did Paul write, "Every Christian ought to obey the civil authorities, for all legitimate authority is derived from God's Authority"?[5] Christians today know as well as anyone that the basic rights and values of our free Western society form a priceless heritage bought by the hallowed sacrifice of thousands and even millions of human beings. The democratic liberties that are so highly esteemed today are actually in large part a Christian achievement, secured by God-fearing men in the face of autocratic and absolute power.[6] They can be preserved only by the vigilance of responsible men and women.

Certainly there are good uses of social power in the world today, though the consideration of them lies outside the scope of this book. One thinks of the quiet, dignified procedure of a high court, robed and in session, listening to testimony, hearing arguments based on a popularly accepted code of justice, considering questions involving the rights and duties of civilized people. Contrast that kind of restrained, deliberative power with the violence of a Timur Lenk (Tamerlane). As Christopher Marlowe describes him, this Mongolian slaughterer of the fourteenth century seems almost to prophesy the atomic warheads of the twentieth.

> I'll bridle all your tongues,
> And bind them close with bits of burnish'd steel,
> Down to the channels of your hateful throats. . . .
> I will, with engines never exercis'd,
> Conquer, sack, and utterly consume
> Your cities and your golden palaces,
> And with the flames that beat against the clouds,
> Incense the heavens, and make the stars to melt. . . .
> And, till by vision or by speech I hear
> Immortal Jove say "Cease, my Tamburlaine,"
> I will persist a terror to the world.[7]

How pleasant and civilized seem our democratic institutions when set alongside the sick, arrogant, mad power hunger of such a primitive conqueror. And yet the pleasantness of the social order in our free nations can be deceptive. Only in the light of history do the true facts emerge. Some of the worst decisions have been handed down by our "best" courts. Some of the most dastardly acts have been committed by well-meaning chiefs of state. The aura of dignity that surrounds those who wield authority is man-made; and man, as the Bible defines him, is a sinner. The early Christians told the authorities of their day, "We ought to obey God rather than men,"[8] and ever since that day Christians have had to balance their attitudes toward human power. On the one hand, they recognize that they are not exempt from the social scene; they have a role to play in observing the laws of the land and building a better world, even if it be only to give out the Gospel while there is time. On the other hand, their judgment of the power game does not change because of

Christian participation. They work for peace where there is no peace, and while they pray for the return of the Prince of Peace.

Meanwhile the natural man sets his goals, and they are always the same: he wants to send in the plays. Such is the aim of the politician as he calls a press conference. It is the intention of the aboriginal witch doctor as he recites his incantations and prepares his brew. It is the object of the distance runner as he grinds out mile after mile in preparation for the Olympic trials. It is the goal of the lobbyist as he casually makes the rounds of the Washington cocktail parties; the goal of the suburban hostess as she draws up her invitation list; the goal of the church executive as he prepares the statistical charts for his annual meeting.

To be the Expert, the Champion, the All-American, the Victor, the Old Pro, the Master, the King, the Kingmaker, Number One, the Gold Medal winner, the Blue Ribbon winner, the new Dolly Madison, Miss America, Miss World, Miss Universe—this, says modern man, is what makes life worth living. This is where it's at.

Unfortunately it is a shimmering lie, as the literature of the day attests. For what if we don't make it? Thomas Wolfe, in a passage in *Look Homeward, Angel*, gives us the picture of a man who was a hopeless loser in the power game but who had been momentarily sold on its soul-destroying philosophy:

I think I'm in hell, thought Eugene, and they say I stink because I have not had a bath. Me! Me! Bruce-Eugene, the Scourge of the Greasers, and the greatest fullback Yale ever had! Marshal Gant, the savior of his country! Ace Gant, the hawk of the sky, the man who brought Richthofen down! Senator Gant, Governor Gant, President Gant, the restorer and uniter of a broken nation, retiring quietly to private life in spite of the weeping protest of one hundred million people, until, like Arthur of Barbarossa, he shall hear again the drums of need and peril.

Jesus-of-Nazareth Gant, mocked, reviled, spat upon, and imprisoned for the sins of others, but nobly silent, preferring death rather than cause pain to the woman he loves. Gant, the Unknown Soldier, the Martyred President, the slain God of Harvest, the Bringer of Good Crops. Duke Gant of

Westmorland, Viscount Pondicherry, twelfth Lord Runnymede, who hunts
for true love, incognito, in Devon and ripe grain. Yes, George-Gordon-
Noel-Byron Gant, carrying the pageant of his bleeding heart through
Europe, François-Villon Gant, and Ahasuerus Gant, and Edward-the-Black-
Prince Gant, Vercingetorix Gant, and Czar-Ivan-the-Terrible Gant. And
Gant, the Olympian Bull; and Hercules Gant; and Gant, the Seductive
Swan; and Ashtaroth and Mumbo-Jumbo Gant.[9]

What is the purpose of the struggle to the top? Is it to attain glory
for its own sake? Not if the Biblical analysis is correct. The Bible
points to pride as being not an end in itself, but a motivator in the
battle for personal power. The laurel wreath—what is that? But the
grasp, the influence, the authority, the right to command, the jurisdiction, the domination; or else the subtle manipulation, the "power
behind the throne"—that is everything. And once the power comes
it tastes sweet as honey, and man is satisfied except for one thing—
he wants more. All the orchestration of man is built around this
theme; and woven into it are the secondary themes of stimulus and
response, of love and hate, of courage and fear, of longing and
fulfillment.

A study of the career of General George S. Patton during World
War II reveals the difference between position and power. After the
Sicilian campaign Patton fell into disgrace over the slapping of two
soldiers. The result was that, as far as the conduct of the war was
concerned, the scintillating but erratic general was apparently put on
the shelf. He became gloomy and despondent. He had rank, staff,
and prestige but no command. His biographer writes, "He feared,
in the absence of any word or even a hint, either from Washington
or Algiers, there were no plans to use him in future operations. This
was designed to be part of his punishment. He was deliberately led
to believe that his usefulness as a combat leader and, worse still, his
whole career were in serious jeopardy."[10] A few months later he was
called to London and given command of the Third Army in the
Normandy campaign. The depression lifted. He was a man again—
that is, a man in charge.

The perennial human scramble to be a Patton, a Caesar, a Catherine the Great, a Richelieu; or else a Svengali, a Dr. Strangelove, or some other powerful type, is easily misunderstood. After all, we are told, ambition is a good thing in a young person. Competition, it is said, brings out strong qualities. So it does; but invariably and inevitably the human struggle is mixed with sin and thereby produces the fruit of sin. Scripture provides profound insight into this process, and a review of the Bible's teaching on the nature of man's sin would make a useful study at this point.

However, I find that thousands of young people are already aware of the sin in the power process and are attempting to "cop out." They are bombarding the gates of knowledge, determined to find some answers to the human predicament. Why can't everyone be friends, they ask. Why do there have to be these dreadful wars? Why can't we make love instead? Why can't we just live together and enjoy this beautiful world? Why do we have to foul it up? Why do we have to destroy ourselves?

Each new generation has asked these questions, but today's youth are asking them in a time of terrible urgency, with the threat of extinction hanging over their poor little planet. It is therefore all-important that we understand the real nature of our predicament: namely, that every human being is locked into the race for power. When we understand it we can see how foolish it is for a head of state to say of another country, "We love the people; it's the government we don't like." That is what Americans are hearing now from Hanoi and Havana. But government is simply the instrument of the people's collective will. Government is the means by which people act, and people act for power. We are afraid of the enemy, so we try to surround him and crush him. For centuries the watchword in ancient Rome was, "Carthage must be destroyed!" Today the natural inclination of self-preservation says to us, "Bomb the neutral targets—some day they may not be neutral."

Carl Gustav Jung, the psychologist, once observed, "It is well known that firearms go off by themselves if only enough of them are together."[11] Some incident takes place and the carnage starts; retaliation is not slow in coming, and overkill wipes out a major part of the population. The survivors come to take away their dead; they wring their hands and cry, "Why did it have to happen?" But they themselves provide the answer, for as soon as the dead are buried and the surviving population has recovered from normal shock, the quest for power starts all over again. Such is the condition of fallen man.

Whatever the name of the power game may be, these chapters aim to show that it is not Fun City. Scattered on the face of the planet are the monuments of man's broken civilizations. He keeps on building his bridges and towers, and he even scratches up the ocean floor and the surface of the moon; but from the viewing ground of nature and history his future appears bleak. Some scientists predict that the last human drama on earth will be a pitiful contest for survival between two emaciated figures struggling over the last scrap of edible food.

> This is the way the world ends
> Not with a bang but a whimper.[12]

Is there then no hope? Has man used up his options? Is there no power from without or within, from below or above, that can save him?

Chapter 4

Jesus Power Defined

If we merely ask for power, we rob the Spirit of his
personality, for he does not give power without himself.[1]
—JAMES R. McINTIRE

COME with me now if you will to a fishing village on the shore of
Lake Gennesaret in Palestine. We shall stand where we can see the
entrance to a little house of tile and mud. A man wearing a simple
robe of Galilean homespun emerges from the entrance. He carries
nothing behind his back. At the doorway he is greeted by a number
of people suffering from various afflictions. He pauses and lays his
hands on some of them. He chats with the children who cluster
about him. Then he steps to the water's edge, climbs into the prow
of a boat, pushes out a few feet, and turns and addresses the multitude.

This man talks to the Galilean people about power. He tells them
that from time immemorial men have tried to push each other
around, but that he has been sent from God to bring in a new
Kingdom with new rules—rules built around himself. "Listen," he
is saying to his followers, "those who are supposed to rule over the
nations wield lordship over them, and the big names exercise authority over them; *but it shall not be so among you.*"[2] He explains that his
divine mission is to enable people to live by learning to love each
other. He knows they cannot do it in their own strength; and so to
make it possible he will impart to them a new and different kind of
power. "Come to me," he says in effect, "and I will give you that
power."

Did he keep his promise? If he had not kept it, the New Testament would not have been written and Christianity would have followed the mystery religions into oblivion. The stake in Gethsemane was the power issue. The stake on Calvary was the power issue. The stake at the tomb was the power issue. "It is to your advantage that I go away," Jesus told his disciples, "for if I do not go away, the Strengthener will not come to you; but if I go, I will send him to you."[3] No wonder the book of Acts reports that after Pentecost the Sanhedrin "took knowledge" of the disciples "that they had been with Jesus." Whatever it was that Jesus died to give them, they had it!

Our aim is to conduct an examination into this power by skirting the edges of it, much as an engineer scientist might conduct an examination before a nuclear blast. The expression "Jesus Power" which we have adopted may create puzzlement and even apprehension, but it says what needs to be said at this hour. The power itself is very ancient. Jesus Power may be defined as God in action; as the Holy Spirit at work. A more formal definition would be: Jesus Power is a supernatural invasion of spiritual power into the social environment, given directly by God to individuals to demonstrate divine love and to meet human need.

Man, as we have seen, knows something about power, so we need to make a clear distinction between Jesus Power and natural power. Many forms of natural power exist today. Physical power is evident in the muscular energy of men and animals, in the kinetic energy of wind and stream, in the heat of the earth and of the sun. But man also recognizes his own mental, psychic, and volitional capabilities as forces able to use physical power through discipline and control.

A power that penetrates our environment from the outside is something else. Man does not perceive it because he lacks the spiritual capacity to apprehend it. He may observe its effects; he may be dimly aware that it is a supernatural force, but he cannot decide what to make of it. It stumps him. He prefers to think it does not exist, so he pretends to ignore it.

The man of spiritual discernment finds such power not just in the

Gospels but all through the Bible. He finds it in the second verse of Genesis at the very inception of the created universe. He meets it in Moses as he presents himself before Pharaoh with a demand that Israel be allowed to go free. He sees it in David standing up to the giant Philistine, in Micaiah facing the four hundred "kept" prophets, in Zechariah thundering out, "Not by human might, nor by human power, but by the power of my Spirit, says the Lord."[4] He sees it in John the Baptist rebuking Herod Antipas for his immorality. But supremely he finds it in the Gospel record associated with the life of Jesus and the early church. Here is the rich, fallow soil that when cultivated will reveal the growth we are seeking.

The Greek text of the New Testament uses two words that are usually translated "power" in the English Bible. They are by no means the only words, but they are the commonest. One is *exousia,* which refers to the power associated with rule, authority, privilege, right, prerogative, dominion, sway, and jurisdiction. The other is *dunamis,* which refers more to might, strength, force, energy, or to what we sometimes call naked power. The Greek makes a valuable distinction between authority and force, and it would help if we had an English equivalent. For example, when people speak of "black power," "Chicano power," "student power," or "woman power," we ought to ask for clarification: "Do you mean *exousia,* authority, or do you mean *dunamis,* force?" Actually most men do not stop to analyze the nature of the power they seek; they simply reach for it. But we are not now analyzing human power, for we are on the track of something infinitely more significant.

Let us look first at *exousia.* Matthew tells us that Jesus taught "as one having authority."[5] The way he spoke impressed his hearers, for his words had a ring different from what they were used to hearing from the scribes. He talked like a natural leader and ruler of men, and his bearing gave power to his words—Jesus Power. He told a paralytic who was brought to him by four friends, "The Son of man has authority on earth to forgive sins."[6] He told his disciples that all authority in the universe had been given to him. He gave special authority to his followers to preach and to heal.[7] "To as many as received him," wrote John, "he gave authority to become sons of God."[8] In his high-priestly prayer Jesus said, "Father . . . you gave him [that is, himself, the Son] authority over all flesh."[9]

The same thought reverberated through the mind of the Apostle Paul as he wrote to the Colossians of Christ's "pre-eminence,"[10] and to the Ephesians of his exaltation "above all authority,"[11] and to the Philippians of the day when "at the name of Jesus every knee [shall] bow"[12] in the whole creation. The Letter to the Hebrews spoke in the same vein of Christ annulling the sway of Satan,[13] and 1 Peter of the "everlasting dominion" of Christ.[14] (In the latter two instances the Greek word is *kratos*.)

When a man goes about speaking with authority, he is going to be challenged sooner or later, not by the people, but by the authorities. For in the world of the power game, authority goes with power. Jesus had no power in the human sense: he repudiated power. He could have had twelve legions of angels at his command, according to his own statement,[15] but he chose a different way. The only power he had was Jesus Power.

To understand the nature of his clash with the power structure of his day, we need to grasp the enormous importance of the authority of human tradition for the conventional ecclesiastical mind. It will help, perhaps, if we take a brief excursion into the world of the sixteenth century. Blaise Pascal, the French Catholic genius and author, has left us some humorous word pictures of the clerical mentality of his day in his anonymous *Provincial Letters*. One such letter dealing with the subject of authority describes an interview with a French monk of the Jesuit order on the subject of moral principles. It should be remembered that the Jesuits held considerable power in France in those days; they set up themselves as authorities on a multitude of moral and spiritual issues. Their manner of drawing distinctions and their custom of handing down minute decisions on matters of conduct was known as casuistry; the men who made such decisions were casuists. Pascal's fifth letter reads:

"How do you manage?" I asked [the monk], "when the Fathers of the Church happen to differ from any of your casuists?"

"You really know very little of the subject," he replied. "The Fathers were good enough for the morality of their own times; but they lived too far back for that of the present age, which is no longer regulated by them, but by the modern casuists. On this Father Cellot, following the famous Reginald, remarks, 'In questions of morals, the modern casuists are to be preferred to the ancient fathers, though those lived nearer to the times of the apostles.' We leave the fathers to those who deal with positive divinity. As for us, who are the directors of conscience, we read very little of them and quote only the modern casuists. There is Father Diana, for instance, a most voluminous writer; he has prefixed to his works a list of his authorities, which amount to 296, and the most ancient of them is only about eighty years old."

"It would appear then," I remarked, "that all these have come into the world since the date of your [Jesuit] Society."

"Thereabouts," he replied.

"That is to say, dear father, on your advent, St. Augustine, St. Chrysostom, St. Ambrose, St. Jerome, and all the rest, insofar as morals are concerned, disappeared from the stage. Would you be so kind as to let me know the names of those modern authors who have succeeded them?"

"A most able and renowned class of men they are," replied the monk. "Their names are Villalobos, Dellacruz, Veracruz, Ugolin, Tambourin, Fernandez, Martinez, Suarez, Henriquez, Vasquez, Lopez, Gomez, Sanchez, Aldretta, Lorca, Quaranta, Scophra, Pedrezza, Cabrezza. . . ."

"O my dear father!" cried I, quite alarmed, "were all these people Christians?"

"How! Christians!" returned the casuist. "Did I not tell you that these are the only writers by whom we now govern Christendom? . . . ."

"What, father! I always thought that we were bound to take the Holy Scripture and the tradition of the church as our only rule, and not your casuists. . . ."

"Goodness!" cried the monk. "I have had occasion to notice, two or three times during our conversation, that you are no great scholastic."[16]

Recently some black Jews went to Israel on tourist visas claiming to be direct descendants of Abraham. Their claim was disputed and they were denied housing and permanent residence by the Israeli government after the religious leadership decided they did not qualify as Jews. The key question put to them was, "What is your authority for your statements?"

According to Mark 11 Jesus was challenged in a similar way. At issue was the authority by which Jesus presumed to teach and act. The clergy were mystified by his assumption of the prerogatives that go with power. They wanted to know what his credentials were. Who comprised his "Henriquez, Lopez, Vasquez, Gomez, and Sanchez"? But Jesus refused to divulge the source of his *exousia;* instead he asked, "Where did John the Baptist get his authority?"

"Well," they replied, "we don't know."

"Right!" said Jesus in effect. "Then there's no need to know about mine either."

The moral authority of Jesus Christ presents a problem to the conventional mind because the human foundation is missing. Jesus claimed the power of such authority, and displayed it. "If you love me, you will keep my commandments," he said.[17] He based his Messianic credentials on the revealed Word of the Old Testament: "If you really believed Moses, you would be bound to believe Me; for it was about Me that he wrote."[18] Nevertheless Jesus left the matter of men's acceptance of his authority to the mystery of the divine will and the working of the human conscience. As the Son of God, he gave his life that men might know the Grace and power of the Father's love; but if the early chapters of the book of Acts teach anything, they teach that spiritual power involves much more than matters of credential and jurisdiction. It is time to move beyond the issue of authority. As a starting point we might simply accept Bertrand Russell's definition of power as "the production of intended effects."[19] To those effects, and the power that produces them in the dimension of the Spirit, we now turn.

Chapter 5

God's Dynamite

Be Thou my battleshield, sword for the fight;
Be Thou my dignity, Thou my delight,
Thou my soul's shelter, Thou my high tower:
Raise Thou me heavenward, O Power of my power.[1]

—ANCIENT IRISH HYMN

WHEN Jesus stood on the Mount of Olives in his resurrection body and told his disciples, "You will receive power," he began the countdown on the biggest explosion in moral history. He launched the Christian church. The word for "power" Jesus used, as it appears in the Greek manuscripts of Luke's Gospel, was *dunamis,* from which we get dynamo, dynamic, dynamite. It means exactly what we think it means: strength inherent in a thing by virtue of its nature, or force which a person exerts. Today the same word could be used to describe an atomic blast, a home run, an earthquake, a palace coup, or any other demonstration of force or might, whether human, natural, or supernatural.

The word used most often for power in the New Testament is *dunamis.* An in-depth study of the various forms of the word would be helpful, but I shall investigate only a few key passages. One important link of power with Scripture is recorded in Mark 12. Jesus was dealing with a double-edged question about a widow who had married seven brothers in succession, according to custom, and then had died and gone to heaven. The questioner wanted to know whose wife she would be in heaven. Jesus knew this was an effort to trap him, but he met the challenge directly: "You err, knowing neither the Scriptures nor the power of God."[2]

What interests here is the coupling of the Bible with celestial power.[3] Century after century, from Hammurabi to Simon Magus to James Pike, men have sought to harness the supernatural to their ends. In doing so they have so often neglected to connect divine power with the authority of written revelation. That way, says Jesus, is error. God acts in his Word, through his Word, according to his Word, but never against his Word. "Is not my word . . . like a hammer which breaks the rock in pieces?"[4] asked the Lord God of Jeremiah. "The word of God is quick, and powerful, and sharper than any twoedged sword,"[5] wrote the author of the Letter to the Hebrews.

A remarkable validation of this relationship between divine power and scriptural truth comes from an unexpected source. In 1967 Adolf A. Berle, after a long career in U.S. Government service, wrote a book about human power in which he drew up what he called certain "natural laws" relating to the subject. I shall be referring to them from time to time in later chapters; here I shall quote only one such "law": "Power is invariably based on a system of ideas or philosophy."[6] The Bible may be neither systematic nor philosophical, but it certainly contains ideas! And it could be said that Berle's principle applies here, for if the spiritual power that the Bible describes is to be released, it can only be in accordance with the ideas and beliefs that the Bible teaches.

The Word of God being inseparable from the power of God, it follows that Scripture can never be reduced to the level of ordinary literature without a corresponding loss of power. In this view, when a historian locates the Old and New Testaments in the same literary stratum as other ancient writing (the apocrypha and pseudepigrapha, for example) he is stating the truth. But when he suggests that all these documents are equally inspired (or uninspired) of God, he errs. The historian has an unimpeachable right to study the documents, but when it comes to passing spiritual judgments he may not be so well qualified. If he ignores the uniquely inspired revelation in the Bible he will be hard put to come up with a rationale for the writing of the sacred books; and he certainly will be without a clue as to why they continue to affect the world.

The word *dunamis* is worked hard in the New Testament. It describes, for instance, the "power of the Highest" that miraculously overshadowed Mary before the birth of Jesus.[7] It defines the power that went out of Jesus to heal the hemorrhaging woman.[8] In the Gospel according to Matthew, what we know as the Lord's Prayer is concluded with the doxology, "Thine is the kingdom, and the power, and the glory, for ever."[9] Theologians have been debating for years as to what Jesus meant precisely by the Kingdom of God; whatever else it was he meant, he most certainly connected it with power. The Apostle Paul told the Corinthian Christians that the Kingdom of God was not "in word [that is, in wordiness], but in power";[10] he told the Romans that Jesus Christ was "declared," or marked out, to be the Son of God "with power."[11] The word is *dunamis.*

When Paul refers to "the gift of the grace of God given me by the [energy] of his power,"[12] he uses *dunamis.* When he tells Timothy that God has "not given us the spirit of fear, but of power, and of love, and of a sound mind,"[13] it is again *dunamis.* What people often call Jesus' "miracles" are referred to in the King James and Revised Standard Versions as "mighty works,"[14] but the word is derived from *dunamis.* They were literally "powers" (that is, "works of power"), according to the Gospel accounts.

At the trial in Caiaphas' house Jesus was asked if he claimed to be the long-expected Messiah, and he replied, according to Mark, "I am; and you will see the Son of man sitting at the right hand of Power."[15] The implications of that verse could provide sermons for a thousand years. The word "power" *(dunamis)* is substituted for the name "God"; therefore Jesus must have considered God and power to be interchangeable expressions; therefore, it would seem, to know God is to know power! Pay a visit to a theological seminary library and scan all the books it contains on the nature and attributes of God. How many of them mention power?

Most of the other references to power as *dunamis* are found in the book of the Acts of the Apostles, the Letters, and the book of Revelation. The Apostle Paul says that he is not ashamed of the Gospel for it is "the saving power of God."[16] He speaks of Christ crucified as "the power of God and the wisdom of God."[17] He adds, "My preaching was not in persuasive words of human wisdom, but in spiritual demonstration and power, that your faith might not be in the wisdom of man but in the power of God."[18]

To the church in Thessalonica Paul wrote that "our glad tidings came to you not in word only but in power and in the Holy Spirit and much assurance."[19] To the Philippians he spoke of the power of the resurrection.[20] To Timothy he wrote that "we are to suffer evils along with the glad tidings according to God's power,"[21] thus suggesting a direct connection between Christian suffering and Jesus Power.[22]

Peter's personal characteristics before the crucifixion are well known: they included impulsiveness, weakness, and vacillation. One of the great scenes in the book of Acts reveals a new Peter, now bold and filled with Jesus Power, pausing at the Gate Beautiful to heal a lame man. He tells the beggar, "Silver and gold have I none [a modern paraphrase might be, "I'm sorry I happen to be broke"]; but such as I have give I thee: In the name of Jesus Christ of Nazareth rise up and walk."[23] (Silver and gold are the poker chips of the human power game; Peter is now operating under a different kind of power.) Later Peter talks about Jesus Power to the crowd in Solomon's porch: "Men, Israelites, why wonder at this? Why look on us so intently as if by our own power or piety we made him walk?"[24] And when the Sanhedrin gathers the next day to investigate the event, and asks Peter and John, "By what power or by what name did you do this?"[25] Peter replies, "In the name of Jesus this man stands before you sound."[26]

Peter was fully aware that Jesus Power was moving through him, but he was also aware of the revolution that had had to take place in his thinking before it could. A magician named Simon, who knew a good thing when he saw it, offered Peter money and said, "Give me this power [here the word is authority, *exousia*], so that anyone I lay my hands on may receive the Holy Spirit." But Peter replied, "No, the thoughts of your heart are not right." And he added, "To hell with your money."[27]

Years later, in his first surviving letter, Peter told the Christians of Asia that they belonged with us "who by the power of God are being guarded through faith for salvation."[28]

Many other New Testament references to power as *dunamis* might be added, but I shall mention only one: the description in the Letter to the Hebrews of "the power of an indestructible life."[29] This passage places Jesus Power in the context of eternity.

The Greeks were not limited to the two words for power. Interchanged with *exousia* and *dunamis* in the New Testament we find the word *kratos,* to which reference has already been made. This signifies the exercise of power and is often translated as strength or might. It sometimes appears in company with *ischus,* another word for power which carries the connotation of God-given ability, or inner strength that determines the use of power. In the magnificent doxology in Revelation 5, *dunamis, kratos,* and *ischus* are all brought into play to describe the power of God:

Worthy is the Lamb that was slain to receive power [*dunamis*], and riches, and wisdom, and strength [*ischus*], and honour, and glory, and blessing. . . . Blessing, and honour, and glory, and power [*kratos*], be unto him that sitteth upon the throne, and unto the Lamb for ever and ever.[30]

Our Greek lesson may not have taught us much, but it has dramatized hopefully the distinction that the New Testament draws between Jesus Power and the kind of power human beings normally use and abuse. Linguistically there is common ground: they share the same vocabulary. Only when we move into the dimension of meaning do we find a great gulf fixed.

We have now earned the right to ask an important question, one
that this book was written to try to answer: What are the criteria of
Jesus Power? What are the signs, the characteristic evidences of this
spiritual phenomenon? Not, certainly, just a great blast of wind (to
use a popular camp-meeting metaphor). Not the sweep of a prairie
fire (to use another). Not simply crowds of people swarming about
a charismatic preacher. Not ecstasy, or miracle, or tithing, or church
growth, or mass baptisms, or Gospel teams, or glossolalia, or nights
in prayer, or "demonstrations," or a sudden increase in Bible sales,
or singing in the subways, or restitutions, or fewer drunks in the
local tank, or any of the measurements by which journalists and
others have commonly sought to detect a spiritual awakening. All of
these evidences may be present and more besides; or none.

As we shall see in the pages that follow, the essential prerequisite
for Jesus Power, according to the New Testament, is the depowering
of man.

Chapter 6

The Depowering of Man

It is not enough for a man to say he is sorry for his sins. His heart must be thoroughly humbled and broken. Then he is fit to be made a vessel of Grace here and of glory hereafter. Do not daub with untempered mortar. Dig deeper, and labor for this humbled and broken heart, and then the heavens shall sooner fail than this shall come to nothing.[1]

—THOMAS HOOKER (1586?–1647)

A few months ago I read the following letter written by a young man who had been brought up in a Christian home:

Oh, if I could just make you see what I am feeling now. I am nothing, nobody, a failure, and my ego is cracking under my failures. I was playing God in the daily events, and couldn't realize why things didn't go the way that I had planned them. I felt this was my life and the other three billion people in the world were here mainly to see that I enjoyed it. I have been living in a Walter Mitty world. What little money I get is spent on me—on whatever I want. A fine man I am. How did I get this way? When did I become God? What a phony I am.[2]

This young person appears to be truly broken. He has run out the string; no longer is he exercising lordship or throwing his weight around. He sees his life crumbling in ruins and has come weeping to the foot of the cross. At the moment there is a total lack of power in his life. It seems appropriate here to introduce another of Adolf Berle's "natural laws": "When there is a power vacuum, it will inevitably be filled."[3] The thought has a familiar ring. Jesus indicated the same thing in describing the unclean spirit that went out of a man, only to return with seven other and deadlier spirits. But in his Sermon on the Mount Jesus also talked about a power vacuum that left man accessible to a new and life-changing influx of God-given strength. The purpose of this chapter is to look into that vacuum.

First, a new word is needed to explain the nature of what has happened. The process (if it be a process) that took place in the life of the young man just cited will obviously not be covered by such verbs as "enervate," "devitalize," "unman," "soften," or "weaken." In the absence of a better term I have chosen to coin the word "depower," meaning "to create a power vacuum." I am sorry that the lexicographers say the word does not exist, for it seems to help explain a spiritual event. The best way I know to interpret it is to quote the opening statement of the Sermon on the Mount: "Blessed are the poor in spirit: for theirs is the kingdom of heaven."[4]

Jesus tells us in these words that God is looking for poverty of spirit. How and when do mortals achieve that quality which he says is blessed of God? When the ground of our self-sufficiency has been removed; when our "give" is gone and we are reduced to a cry of dereliction such as Jesus uttered at the cross. Poverty of spirit means the way of the cross. It is not a velvet carpet for a prince of the church.[5] It is a poor way: a way unfriendly and deserted, soiled with blood, toil, tears, and sweat; a way that breaks down a man's spiritual vitality and leaves him at the end of his tether. We think God is looking for spiritual maturity, for spiritual giants, but Jesus says No; he is looking for spiritual dwarfs, for those who are poor in spirit. He is looking for unprofitable servants.

Roy Hession draws a graphic picture of Isaiah's "highway of holiness" in the book *Calvary Road*. He tells us:

The only way onto the Highway is up a small, dark, forbidding hill—the Hill of Calvary. It is the sort of hill we have to climb on our hands and knees —especially our knees. . . . At the top of the hill, guarding the way to the

Highway, stands the Cross. At the foot of the Cross is a low door, so low
that to go through it one has to stoop and crawl. It is the only entrance to
the Highway. We must go through it if we would go any farther. The door
is called the Door of the Broken Ones. Before we can enter the Highway,
God must bend and break that stiff-necked self so that Christ reigns in its
stead.[6]

There is no other way for God to work. He cannot fill our
cups with the water of life until they have been drained of all
other waters. That is why the blessed ones are those who are
poor in spirit. That is why the street people of our own day
often become vital and radiant Christians. It is their very poverty
and insolvency that gives them the capacity for taking on treasure. It is their powerlessness that makes them eligible for divine
empowerment. When Paul was afflicted by a thorn in the flesh,
he was told by his Lord, "The strength [*dunamis*] is fulfilled in
weakness [*astheneia*]."[7] Dwight L. Moody points to the impossible alternative: "If God were to endue us with power when we
are filled with conceit, we would become as vain as peacocks,
and there would be no living with us."[8]

To go up Calvary road on our knees is a humiliating, painful,
groveling experience. It teaches us that not only have we no power
(dunamis) before God; we do not even have any rights *(exousia)*. But
that's what it means to be broken. To go to the cross is to become
a candidate for the power of the resurrection. When we have no
spirit at all, we are ready to receive the blessing and gift and power
of the Holy Spirit and the promise of the Kingdom of Heaven. To
put it another way, we cannot make it under our own power, but in
his power we can go all the way. That is what Jesus taught in the first
Beatitude.

Now it is all very well to tell a man that he must lay down his
private scepter and become an empty vessel; that he must prostrate
his life before the altar of God. But what then? What does the Lord
say to the young man who has come weeping to kneel before him?
Does he say, "On your feet, old boy! Buck up! Play the man! It isn't

all that bad. The world is full of opportunity; try a little grit, grace, and gumption, and see if you don't make out fine!''

No. That is what men say because they don't know what else to say. Even while men say it they don't believe it. They know what life is. They know it is a power game in which the casualties are heavy. And because they don't like to see another casualty—particularly a young one—they pretend to be cheerful. The truth is that men fear a power vacuum; they fear the seven demons who may come back with the demon who left; and so when a crisis occurs they try to fill it. In this, nations are not different from individuals; a national leader dies and immediately a power vacuum is created in the land. Instinct requires that it be filled, and quickly. So the people shout, ''The king is dead; long live the king.'' Before the body is cold a struggle may erupt to take over the leadership.

What Jesus says to the man who comes to him is, ''If any man would follow after me, let him deny himself and take up his cross and follow me.''[9] He does not issue a manual of instructions or chart a crash program; he points to the heavenly Father and talks about prayer. Jesus faced many crises, and he dealt with all of them in prayer. When the time arrived he met each situation with complete mastery.

At the end of his life, when he was ready to ascend to his Father, Jesus did not try to organize his followers into an institution. He did not convene a planning conference to carry out his wishes with a prescribed course of action. Instead he told them to go back to Jerusalem and do nothing. His actual instructions were to ''remain in Jerusalem until you are clothed with power [*dunamis*] from on high.''[10] The same command was repeated in Acts 1; Luke reports that Jesus charged his disciples not to leave the city, but to await the promise of the Father which they had heard from his lips. They were to tarry until they were baptized with the Holy Spirit. ''You will receive power,'' he said. ''The Holy Spirit will come upon you, and you will be witnesses to me to the ends of the earth.''[11]

We have seen that when a man discovers what the power game

has done to his soul, and retreats from it, a vacuum is created. We have noticed Berle's warning that where there is a power vacuum it will invariably be filled. Man dreads chaos in his life, so he casts about to fill it with something; but now we learn that if he waits for God, God will fill it. Harold Ockenga says that waiting is necessary for a Christian to reach "a point of despair" in himself, so "he will depend upon God to do something in his life."[12] Jesus says, "Wait for the power from on high. Wait for my power."

Ah, but we don't like that tarrying bit. To wait around is not the red-blooded Western way. We want to be out on the battlefield for our Lord; we want to fire up the boilers and get going. Or to switch to a figure of the seventies, we would rather be saved in a Lincoln Continental without even taking our foot off the accelerator. We would simply switch lanes in the freeway and turn at the interchange and blink our headlights to let God know we're now on his side.

Here is an aspiring pop singer. He goes to a Jesus rally, listens to a Christian evangelist; and even while he is deciding to make a change in his life, he is thinking in his heart, "I'll just take my instrument and go around the world singing to great audiences for Jesus, and to God be the glory." Here is an aspiring author who reads a paperback by some fine Christian writer like Catherine Marshall. He is touched. He puts down the book, bows his head and says, "I'm going to get converted. Then maybe I can knock out a best seller with my picture on the back cover, and to God be the glory." Here is a young salesman who comes to an evangelistic crusade and hears Billy Graham. He walks down on to the stadium turf, repeats the sinner's prayer, and thinks within himself, "I have a good set of lungs; I can talk as well as Billy can. Now instead of selling fortified dog food I'll take a couple of semesters of Bible school, and then go out and preach to vast crowds and stay at the Holiday Inn, and to God be the glory."

Oh, no, you don't. Saul of Tarsus had some ideas about preaching the Gospel to the Gentiles almost as soon as he got back on the road for Damascus, but the Lord had other ideas. He sent Paul into the

Arabian desert for three years to shake him down. You don't cab into the Jesus Motel! You take off your shoes and crawl up the rocky hill to the cross; and then you go through what every believer has to experience. You go back to Jerusalem on foot and wait for God to act. You fall on your face with Ezekiel and John and a few thousand others. Don't ask me what to do! You do nothing. You get depowered; that comes first. Only then can the power come from on high.

Chapter 7

Plan A and Plan B

> I would not have you pitch upon me as the man able to
> answer doubts. . . . My cracked dish and leaky vessel can
> hold little of Christ Jesus. . . . It is no pride for a drowning
> man to catch hold of a rock. . . . Yet it pleases the Spirit
> of Jesus to blow his sweet wind through a piece of dry
> stick, that the empty reed may keep no glory to itself.[1]
> —SAMUEL RUTHERFORD (1600?–1661)

LIFE offers us two package arrangements for our time on earth: Plan
A and Plan B. Under Plan A (which Jesus warns against) we go for
the top and end up on the bottom. Under Plan B (which is his plan)
we line up last and wind up first.

Plan A calls for the seizing of power and holding it. It was a plan
apparently first devised by Satan and it led to his expulsion from
heaven. Adam adapted the plan to human purposes and turned it
into a power play in the Garden of Eden. His gamble did not pay
off; he lost everything and became a frustrated wanderer on the face
of the earth. But he continued to work at Plan A because, like a
hooked plunger, he was never convinced that he had really lost the
power game. As Machiavelli once said, "The desire to acquire
possessions is a very natural and ordinary thing."[2]

Plan B works on a different basis. It calls for the renunciation of
human power rather than its acquisition. Jesus set up the plan and
furnished the potential to make it work; but he refused to allow his
fuel to be mixed with any other kind—and for a very good reason.
Leon Morris remarks, "When we know that the power that comes

into our hearts and lives is not the power of any creature, but that of none less than God himself, it makes all the difference."[3]

Jesus Power is given to us not for our own use, to augment our own situation; it is given only for God's use, to accomplish his purpose. God's purpose is to bring men to himself—not into this or that church, or this or that movement or school of thought, but to himself. As Samuel Chadwick says, God does not let out his attributes.[4] His power cannot be detached from his presence. Jesus Power is inseparable from Jesus. God is not simply the giver of power, he wields it. And since it is his power that is at work, we dare not touch it; we might better touch forked lightning. J. Stuart Holden, the British preacher, writes:

God does not invest a man with power for any other work than that of the Kingdom, and no man who does not renounce all forms of leadership other than spiritual can ever know the enduement of a personal Pentecost. There must be a complete separation to the divine purpose for which power is bestowed.[5]

Jesus' teaching persuaded many of his hearers, but not all. In some cases confusion resulted from a misunderstanding of his attitude toward power. His own disciples found it hard to believe him when he told them in effect, "The big wheels run over everybody in their path, but it shall not be so among you."[6] The multitudes did not believe him when he declared, "Whoever wants to become great among you shall be your servant, and whoever wants to be first shall be your slave."[7]

Peter did not understand. When Jesus predicted his own coming suffering and rejection and death, Peter protested, saying he would not allow his Master to go through such an ordeal. Jesus rebuked him sharply. He told Peter his thoughts were of the things of men, not the things of God.

James and John did not understand. They got into an argument one day over priority of position in the future Kingdom of Heaven —much to the disgust of the other disciples. Even Jesus found it hard to conceal his annoyance at their jockeying. Jesus told them he could do nothing for them as he was not in charge of the seating arrangements in glory. However, he could promise them a baptism of fire.

The rich young ruler did not understand. Jesus told him to get rid of the trappings of the power game and he went away sorrowing. He had been struggling to keep the commandments of God under Plan A; when Jesus offered him a simpler plan he passed it up.

The brothers who asked Jesus to settle a family argument did not understand. The dispute was over inheritance, which is another name for human power. Jesus refused to touch the matter.

Pontius Pilate did not understand. His career operated under Plan A and he knew nothing of Plan B. Jesus told him that even Plan A lay under the overarching sovereignty of God; that he, Pilate, would have no authority at all unless God had given it to him. So much for the validity of the Roman Empire.

Herod Antipas did not understand. He thought that political power was all there was, and that the way to it was through political intrigue. Jesus called him a fox.

The religious authorities of Israel did not understand. To them, as to religious hierarchies generally, Jesus was a maverick. He showed no interest in gaining ecclesiastical power by going through the rabbinical chairs. He expressed contempt for religious types who used their piety to claim status and authority among men.

The mob at Golgotha did not understand. Jesus had already said that if he chose he could call upon his Father, who would furnish him with twelve legions of angels. The mob wanted him to "save himself and come down from the cross." All that would have been Plan A. He chose Plan B.

Today's man of the world does not understand. He has one great aim in life: to join the power elite. To arrive at that plateau he may stoop to guile, cheating, and grasping in the Machiavellian tradition. Jesus warned however that the power game would destroy a man. He said, "Unless you repent, you will all perish."[8]

God's alternative to the power game is Plan B. It calls for the depowering of man, as we have seen, but it goes further. As I understand the meaning of Christian experience, each of us has to recapitulate in a sense what the disciples did between the Ascension and Pentecost. Before we can receive power, each of us has to "go to Jerusalem" and wait for Deity to act. God keeps his own time; he maintains his own schedule; and there is nothing automatic about his giving of power. When we have emptied ourselves he will come in; but at his discretion and pleasure. That is why "tarrying" is important. As Ralph W. Harris says, "Tarrying is an attitude of the heart, will and mind, rather than certain actions."[9] As we wait upon the Lord, we adjust to his schedule, and when we do, we shall be baptized by the Holy Spirit. "You *will* receive power," said Jesus. There will be no slipup.

Why do we have to go through all the embarrassment and humiliation of being depowered before God will route his power through us? Paul gives the best answer: "We have this treasure [the treasure of the Gospel] in earthen vessels [bowls of clay, or better, mud], that the excellency of the power [*dunamis*] may be of God, and not of us."[10] God will not give his glory to another. He maintains the royal prerogative. Then when the power comes, when the Holy Spirit enters a man and takes up his dwelling place there, it becomes the most exciting, elevating experience known to mortals. The same young man who was quoted at the beginning of the last chapter was able to say publicly six weeks later:

I had to take that pride and move it aside, destroy it, forget it, before I could find Jesus Christ. For without God we're nothing, nobody is anything. For this last month I have felt a joy, a happiness, an exhilaration, and a new kind of outlook on life. I see things that I never saw before. I can't possibly tell you how great it is to be a member of Christ's church, just to love God. It's so exciting that I just wish you yourself could find this true happiness that comes when you put your own pride, your own ego, into perspective with your own life, and with God, and come as a child to meet Jesus Christ and be born again.[11]

Amazing? Yes. Exceptional? No. I have seen hundreds of similar letters from new Christians, and the process is always the same: first the emptying, then the filling. First the confession of sin, then the experience of the new birth and redemption through Jesus Christ.

Earlier I mentioned a number of people in the New Testament who did not understand Jesus' teaching about power. I do not imply that such misunderstanding was general, for many who listened caught the Master's meaning. God's truth is not all that obscure. Scripture displays its essential unity to the inquiring mind as it treats the power question. Book after book in Old and New Testament alike attests to the same truth: "The race is not to the swift, nor the battle to the strong."[12]

Job, a man of means and power, encounters a series of personal disasters and begins tossing hard questions at the Almighty. He is slapped down by a magnificent delineation of God's power—perhaps the greatest in all of literature. Job gets his only answer out of the whirlwind: "Where wast thou when I laid the foundations of the earth?"[13] At the end of the lengthy divine soliloquy, Job makes his response, and the Christian believer recognizes it as authentic: "Behold, I am vile; what shall I answer thee? . . . . I know that thou canst do everything. . . . therefore have I uttered that I understood not. . . . Wherefore I abhor myself, and repent in dust and ashes."[14] The Almighty responds in turn and gives Job twice as much as he had before.

Moses is a fugitive from justice roaming the "back side of the desert" with a price on his head and saddled with a criminal record, a speech impediment, an unpleasant disposition, and a bad reputation with Egyptian and Hebrew alike. Shorn of the royal authority he knew in Egypt, he meets the holy God in the burning bush. Equipped now with the divine power, Moses is a loser no longer; he becomes the emancipator of his race and the greatest lawgiver in human history.

David hides from King Saul in the cave of Adullam and gathers to himself every bankrupt malcontent in Palestine. Because they are powerless these men are ready for anything, even for God. David emerges as Israel's king and greatest hero.

Jonah finds himself pitched overboard in mid-ocean, two fathoms under water, with seaweed wrapped around his head. With his last breath he prays. God sends power. Jonah is rescued and becomes the instrument to bring revival to a great city.

John the Baptist is a nobody who spends his days wandering in prayer in the desert near Jericho. He is reduced to wearing animal skins and catching and eating locusts. Yet this man knows his Scripture, and God sends power. Crowds flock to hear John at the Jordan. He identifies Jesus as the Messiah and attacks the sins of the nation. Jesus praises him as the greatest of the prophets.

The friendly Roman centurion, seeking healing for his slave, places the spiritual authority of Jesus over his own "unworthy" power. Roman power submits to Jesus Power; the slave is healed.

Mary is a provincial peasant girl living in the hills of Galilee, far from the seats of the mighty; yet she is the one divinely chosen to give birth to the Son of God. She then prophesies that the mighty will be pulled down from their seats, that those of low degree may be exalted. Concerning Jesus she tells the servants at the Cana wedding, "Do whatever he tells you."[15]

A wise Scottish woman once told me, "A saint is a person who knows how to get out of God's way." The statement is not definitive but it will do for a start. We have seen that the Bible is filled with illustrations of people who have chosen either Plan A or Plan B. Peter tried to choose both and consequently fell between two stools, and the Gospel writers record that he "went out and wept bitterly." Similar tears have been shed by many Christians who have tried to keep a mailing address on Straight Street while conducting a business on Broadway. It won't work. No one can operate Plan A and Plan B simultaneously; one of them has to be abandoned. Yet to give up the power game is difficult; like Peter, we are tempted to think we can do God more good if we are in his way than if we are out of it. Campbell Morgan says,

It is easy to speak of abandonment, and yet it is the one thing from which all men shrink. They are quite prepared to sign pledges and even cheques, and to do any amount of work, if only God will let them have their own way in some part of their lives. If only God will not bring them to the cross, they will do anything; but they draw back from the place of death. Yet it is only in that place that the Holy Spirit is able to flow out into every part of the life and energize it.[16]

Again we note that expression, "the Holy Spirit." The time has come in our search for Jesus Power to inquire more fully of this Person, about whom we have heard so much and seem to know so little.

Chapter 8

The Spirit of Power

> Sir, the pretending to extraordinary revelations and gifts
> of the Holy Ghost is a horrid thing; yes, sir, it is a very
> horrid thing. Sir, you have no business here; you are not
> commissioned to preach in this diocese; therefore I ad-
> vise you to go hence.[1]
> > —BISHOP JOSEPH BUTLER TO JOHN WESLEY
> > (in Bristol, England, 1738)

JESUS Power is not some kind of exalted religious feeling that people get, or a holy influence wafting through the church corridors. Jesus Power is simply another way of speaking of God the Holy Spirit, who is God in action.

Like millions of people I grew up in a church that did not know quite what to make of the Holy Spirit. The words had a spooky, churchy, mystical sound to me, sometimes even a pleasant sound, for they usually came at the end of the benediction. My experience would certainly uphold A. W. Tozer's contention that "the idea of the Spirit held by the average church member is so vague as to be nearly nonexistent."[2] If the communion of the Holy Spirit (one of those churchy phrases) meant anything to me, it meant freedom to look for spiritual truth and to interpret it any way I wanted. Other churches that talked a lot about the Holy Spirit I avoided as rather "queer."

Today as a Spirit-baptized person I consider the Holy Spirit to be the key to the church's life because he is the key to power. Not religious power, not psychological power, not occult power, but

Jesus Power. Says Samuel Chadwick,

The Holy Spirit is the active, administrative agent of the glorified Son. He is the Paraclete, the Deputy, the acting representative of the ascended Christ. His mission is to glorify Christ by perpetuating his character, establishing his Kingdom, and accomplishing his redeeming purpose in the world. The church is the body of Christ, and the Spirit is the Spirit of Christ. He calls and distributes, controls and guides, inspires and strengthens.[3]

In theological terms the Holy Spirit is the third Person of the Trinity. I confess to very little knowledge of the personality of the Godhead; as Billy Graham says, "This is a mystery we will never be able to understand."[4] God dwelleth in light unapproachable, and is known only as he chooses to reveal himself. The Bible is for Christians the vehicle of his revelation, and the Bible tells us that God is Spirit, and that the Spirit of God is a person. But right now we are in trouble, for twice in the eighth chapter of Romans the Spirit is referred to by the Greek neuter pronoun "it"; and how can "it" be a person?

The best answer I have found is in Leon Morris' volume, *Spirit of the Living God.* He explains:

In English gender is a simple affair. Nouns referring to the masculine sex are masculine, to the feminine sex are feminine. All the rest are neuter. It is beautifully simple. But it is not so in other languages. In Latin, for example, a table is feminine, and we must call it "she." In German a maiden is neuter and should be called "it." In French a hat is masculine and must be referred to as "he." It is all very confusing. Now, in Greek the word for "Spirit" is neuter, and should in strict grammar be referred to as "It." When John uses a pronoun to refer to "Spirit" and the two words are close together, he usually respects his grammar and uses the correct form "It." But if a word or two intervenes he nearly always uses the masculine form "He." This is grammatically incorrect but most illuminating. The explanation is surely that John habitually thought of the Spirit in personal terms, as "He" rather than as "It."[5]

When we speak of the power of the Holy Spirit, therefore, we are speaking not of some "it," a mystical blue light or spiritual electric current that sends vibrations into people. We are speaking of the presence of God himself. From the Scriptures we can adduce certain characteristics of the Spirit of God.

1. He takes the things of Jesus Christ and brings them to our remembrance.

2. He witnesses to the second Person of the Trinity, the Lord Jesus Christ, never to himself.

3. He always speaks the truth because he is the Spirit of Truth.

4. He convicts men of sin and draws them in love to Jesus Christ.

5. He makes the Holy Scripture a living book by inspiring (God-breathing) it from beginning to end.

6. He was active in the creation of the universe.

7. He brought the church into being and sustains it today by his gifts and his power.

8. That power is as mighty and as available to men today as at any time in history.

9. He will not always be present with men.

10. No man can say Jesus is Lord but by the Holy Spirit.

We can understand from Scripture who the Holy Spirit is and what he does, but we cannot penetrate deeper. To know how or why he acts as he does is beyond our ken. "The wind bloweth where it listeth."[6] Bernard Ramm warns, "Any proposed psychological or sociological studies of the workings or operations of the Holy Spirit are meaningless and preposterous. Any attempt to lift the curtain will achieve exactly nothing. Yet this hidden one is the power of God."[7]

The best we can do is to examine some of the terms used to describe the Holy Spirit. He has been called the Spirit of Christ, the Spirit of Truth, the Spirit of Power, the Spirit of Wisdom, among others. He also has been called the Holy Ghost, a term that has confused some people today because the meaning of the term "ghost" has changed in the 360 years since the translation of the King James Bible. Back in 1611, when Shakespeare was still writing, the word "ghostly" meant what we today mean by "spiritual," while the word "spirit" in Shakespeare's day meant what we mean today by a "ghost." Thus it was correct for seventeenth-century Englishmen to speak of the Holy Ghost, just as it is correct for us today to speak of the Holy Spirit. And since both words translate the same Greek word *(pneuma),* neither one can be considered superior to the other.

Now let us look at a common New Testament term used to designate the Holy Spirit: *Paraclete.* This Greek word is a combination of *para,* meaning "from," "by," or "along," and *kletos,* meaning "called" or "invited." The Paraclete is mentioned four times in John 14—16, and the word is traditionally rendered "Comforter," as in John 14:16, "I will pray the Father, and he shall give you another Comforter."

In the First Letter of John the same Greek word is used with a slightly different meaning attached to it. John writes, "If any man sin, we have an advocate [*paracletos*] with the Father, Jesus Christ the righteous."[8] Christ is the Paraclete who stands before God and pleads the cause of man. Yet neither Advocate nor Comforter fully expresses the meaning of Paraclete; they only bring out different aspects of the word. As I have indicated, Paraclete means literally one who is called for or called alongside. A man is in trouble and he sends for assistance; the person who responds is the "called-for one," the Paraclete. He stands beside the one in need and takes his part. In a modern colloquialism one might say, "He bails him out."

Jesus said of the Paraclete in John 14—16 that he will teach, he will bear witness, he will convict, and he will guide. Obviously one who does these things is more than a Comforter or Consoler; he is better described as an Encourager, a Helper or Supporter. The thought of replacement is also present, for Jesus tells us that the

Person and operation of the Holy Spirit will compensate us for his own departure in the flesh. In all these activities the implication of spiritual power is present. As a coach motivates an athletic team and its individual players, so the Holy Spirit motivates the fellowship of believers and the individual Christians.

The Christian who lives by Jesus Power is one who walks in the Spirit, lives in the Spirit, loves in the Spirit, prays in the Spirit, witnesses in the Spirit, and grows in the Spirit. Such activity, however, does not necessarily distinguish him at first glance from other men and women. Christians are known by their love rather than by their life style. The Spirit-filled man will avoid those aspects of his appearance and behavior that are offensive to the Spirit, but he will not make a big production of his avoidance. Prayer habits, linguistic habits, dress habits, political habits, are relative matters to the Spirit of God. Jesus runs a power generator, not an inquisition.

Says Campbell Morgan:

No man can do the work of God until he have the Holy Spirit and is endued with power. It is impossible to preach the Gospel save in the power of the Spirit, because none can comprehend the true meaning of the cross of Christ unless taught by the Spirit of God. Nothing short of the immediate, direct, personal illumination of the Spirit is sufficient equipment. Let all be yielded to the fire and power of the Spirit for cleansing and energy, and the pulpit will be the greatest force in all human life, and every organization of the church will throb and pulsate with divine energy.[9]

The first place in which a believer senses Jesus Power is in his own prayer life. Before conversion he was perhaps shy, reserved, modest, decorous, thinking it more seemly to let others pray, as his behavior would then be less inconsistent in view of his somewhat-less-than-holy daily life. Or he was embarrassed, tongue-tied, overcome by the consciousness of his very real sins. Now as a Christian he is naturally as shy as ever, and as conscious of his shortcomings as ever, but he is made bold by the assurance of forgiveness and the infusion of spiritual power. He is eager to pray, glad to call upon the name of the Lord; he has found a vocabulary and an ability to use it that he never dreamed possible.

When Jesus Power is operating, the Spirit of God does not just hear a man's prayer, he prays through the man and then answers his own prayer. This is humanly speaking a contradiction in set terms, but what is impossible with men is possible with God.

The Holy Spirit helps us with our daily problems and in our praying. For we don't even know what we should pray for, nor how to pray as we should; but the Holy Spirit prays for us with such feeling that it cannot be expressed in words. And the Father who knows all hearts knows, of course, what the Spirit is saying as he pleads for us in harmony with God's own will.[10]

Where such activity takes place, whether it be in a church, a home, a commune, an office, a barracks, or on a raft in mid-ocean, Jesus Power is coming through. Unfortunately a great deal of the praying going on today is of a different order. It is work, hard work, man-made work. People pray literally from exhaustion. They pray because they feel it is their duty, because their mothers told them to, because they are worried and anxious and in trouble. Such prayers are bathed in perspiration, and most of their petitions could be answered by either a grant of money or a kind friend.

As a first-year student in theological seminary I was once required to take a course in "religious education." We were taught that there are five types of praying: adoration, confession, thanksgiving, supplication, submission. These were gathered into an acronym for easy memory: ACTSS. Nothing was said about God's answers to prayer, for in the five steps the whole activity seemed to be man-centered, man-powered, man-controlled. Our study of prayer was wearisome and discouraging. I have since learned that the one element needed to put praying into orbit is Jesus Power, for when the Holy Spirit is monitoring the prayer, things begin to happen.

In addition to leaving out God's participation in the prayer dialogue, our ACTSS formula neglected an important aspect of the human side: intercession, or praying for others.

One of the great men of prayer of this century was a Welsh Bible teacher whose life story was written by Norman P. Grubb and published under the title, *Rees Howells, Intercessor.*[11] That volume has changed the direction of many lives, including my own. I have made a pilgrimage to Llandrindod Wells in Wales and have visited the church where this rough coal miner first sensed the touch of the Holy Spirit upon his life. He later founded a Bible college that is still flourishing. "The meaning of prayer," Howells used to say, "is answer." Not long after his conversion he engaged in a life of personal intercession for specific individuals. He said God had told him he was no longer to pray at his own whim or fancy, but only to pray those prayers that the Holy Spirit gave him. "The power," Howells explained to Grubb, "is in Christ. As the intercessor remains united to Christ and abiding in him, Christ's power operates through the intercessor and accomplishes what needs to be done." In one remarkable instance Howells was told that he did not need to pray for a particular person's salvation any longer; that the answer had been given, and "it was now a case of praising before the victory." Six weeks later the person was converted.

Rees Howells showed me for the first time what prayer can do when it is taken seriously and is backed by Jesus Power. I have often heard it said that "prayerlessness breeds powerlessness," but I think the slogan could well be turned around: "Powerlessness breeds prayerlessness." People become disheartened when their praying seems to get nowhere, but when the Holy Spirit takes over the praying chores it is a different matter. God begins to work. Prayers not only "get through," they come back—with answers.

There is much we do not know about prayer, particularly about praying in the Spirit; but perhaps we can begin making prayer real by weeding out a lot of general praying that has no cutting edge. We can ask the Holy Spirit to remove the obstructions in our own lives that are keeping the answers from coming through loud and clear. We can make our prayers more specific, using names, setting goals, keeping lists. As we learn to pray in faith, believing, the answers will certainly come.

Today the Holy Spirit is conducting the greatest monopoly in the universe. He is engaged in bringing people to God and filling them with Jesus Power. He has a monopoly because no one else is doing it or can do it. He uses the church for his purpose wherever and whenever the church places itself at his disposal. How important is the activity and presence of the Holy Spirit to the life of a local congregation, W. A. Criswell has clearly indicated.

Without the presence of the Spirit there is no conviction, no regeneration, no sanctification, no cleansing, no acceptable works. We can pray without him, but our prayers do not reach beyond the sound of our voices. We can preach without him, but our sermons fall to the ground. We can sing without him, but our melodies are hollow and meaningless. We can perform duties without him, but our service is dull and mechanical. Life is in the quickening Spirit.[12]

To understand the ministry of the Spirit of God in the church, let us examine two more "laws of power" laid down by Adolf Berle: "Power is exercised through, and depends on, institutions," and, "Power . . . invariably . . . acts in . . . a field of responsibility."[13] If it be true, as the Bible indicates, that the church is God's chosen instrument for channeling his power to humanity, then it would seem that the church has a clearly defined "field of responsibility." Its prime mission is not to take a stand on every ambiguous social issue of the day but to win souls; that is, to minister to human need by delivering its redemptive product—spiritual power.

God is a miracle-working God. Both the Old and New Testaments are filled with stories of mighty acts wrought by men and women in the power of the Spirit. Samson, David, Elijah, Elisha, Deborah, all knew the Spirit's power; and above all, Jesus Christ used that power to heal the blind, the lame, the deaf, and the dumb, and to raise the dead. The New Testament makes it clear that the followers of Jesus were also to be known by their deeds; that their witness was to be "confirmed" by "signs following."[14] The book of the Acts of the Apostles records many such evidences of spiritual power in the history of the early church. The Apostle Paul wrote to the Christians at Corinth that his testimony among them was not just preaching "in persuasive words of human wisdom, but in demonstration of the Spirit and of power."[15]

C. S. Lewis has shown in a convincing tour de force of logic that what scientists call the "uniformity of nature" is not a fact of experience at all. It is a subjective conviction which, he says, men hold and cherish because anything else would be detestable to them. In fact, Lewis claims our very repugnance toward a disorderly universe "is derived from Nature's Creator and ours." But once we admit God, he warns us, we have no security against miracle. That is the risk we take.[16] I do not believe the age of miracles has passed. In these pages there has been no discussion of the sovereignty of the Holy Spirit over nature, for the same reason that there has been no attempt to classify the Holy Spirit's various gifts and dispensations to men.[17] Our concern is limited to the general field of divine power as it relates to mankind. Men and women want to know what Jesus Power is and how they can get it. The Bible teaches that spiritual power is manifested through miracles and also through special gifts; but the verse that tells me more about Jesus Power perhaps than any other is found in Ephesians 3:

Now unto him that is able to do exceeding abundantly above all that we ask or think, according to the power that worketh in us. . . .[18]

In us! Making all allowance for the mighty display of divine power that created the universe and has sustained it for perhaps billions of years; that brought life into being, fashioned man in God's image, defeated evil at the cross, and broke the bands of death, I come back to this verse. It tells of God's power at work in puny, timid, unimpressive, ill-equipped men. I see it illustrated in a sorry band of fishermen and tax collectors who were suddenly fused into courageous instruments of divine design.

Lord, give us that power. Give us that water to drink. Give us that bread to eat. Come into our lives and make them mighty for You, in Jesus' name.

Chapter 9

The Great Power Failure

Sometimes people will stand up in a meeting and say, "I am trying to serve God in my poor, weak way." Well, if you are trying to serve God in your poor, weak way, quit it. Your duty is to serve God in his strong, triumphant way.[1]

—REUBEN A. TORREY (1856–1928)

THE Gospel writers dwell at more length than usual on an incident that took place at the foot of the Mount of Transfiguration after Jesus descended from the summit. According to the synoptic account, a man stepped out of the crowd and begged his help for an only child who was suffering from convulsions. The man told Jesus that he had already asked the disciples to cast out the evil spirit that was afflicting his boy, but they had been unable to do so.

Jesus then rebuked the spirit and healed the child. Luke commented, "And they were all amazed at the mighty power of God."[2] (The Greek word he used for "power" is none of those we have been examining, but *megaleiotes,* which could be translated the "majesty" or "magnificence" of God.) Then afterward, Matthew added, the disciples came to Jesus privately and asked, "What happened? Why were we not able to cast out the demon?"[3]

And there in miniscule is the history of the Christian church. *What happened to the Jesus Power?*

Already Jesus had called his disciples by name, instructed them, commissioned them, and sent them out to preach and to heal. He had told them that they would do greater things than he had done.

But when the crunch came, in this instance, they couldn't deliver.

If we take a tour through twenty centuries of church history we find that again and again, at the very time Jesus Power was needed, it was missing. Power was available—plenty of it: military power, inquisitorial power, hierarchical power, political power, dictatorial power, all operating under the clerical robes. Thank God it was not always used; power in the church was not always coercive. Here and there, in unusual ways and unexpected places, and many times under a cloak of quietness, Jesus Power could be found. It was beautiful to watch—but hard to find.

Today the names of the heroes and heroines of the Christian faith are familiar to many of us. Preachers, teachers, evangelists, missionaries, churchmen, and churchwomen who obviously knew Jesus and drew upon his power have inspired the whole world. Too often they have been portrayed wearing haloes, as if there were something superhuman about them. To make a Christian into something other than a man or a woman is an anthropological gaffe. The heroes of Christianity have been ordinary mortals shaped like ourselves. What made them extraordinary was what God poured into them.

Why have there not been more such people? It is a dangerous question, for ultimately it can be answered only by the person who asks it. In any case we learn more from our failures than we do from our successes. On the night of November 9, 1965, New York City and much of the surrounding Atlantic seaboard was blacked out by the failure of electric power. An overloaded relay station near Toronto, Ontario created a short circuit, and the power failure leaped from one station to another. A feeling exists among many observers that something like it is taking place in the spiritual life of the Western world today. Reports from western Europe, Canada, Australia, and the United States all convey the same information: people are leaving the churches. A popular American book is entitled *The Last Years of the Church*; when it appeared the *New York Times* hailed it as "provocative, penetrating, exciting." (By contrast,

another book even more recent—and more exciting—has the title
Why Conservative Churches Are Growing.)

In his famous commentary on Romans Karl Barth pictures a dry
canal, calling it "the impression of divine revelation left behind in
time." In a past generation and under different conditions, he says,
this canal was "filled with the living water of faith and of clear
perception."[4] But the days when the water of Biblical revelation
coursed through it have vanished; now the canal is empty and dry.
The people who live on its banks still cling to the memory—the law
—but are no longer witnesses to the power.

It is not the first time that the church has sensed a loss of supernatural power in its ministry. Paul wrote to Timothy warning of apostates
who would enter the church "having a form of godliness, but denying the power thereof."[5] John wrote from Patmos to the church in
Ephesus, "I have this against you, that you left your first love. Recognize your condition, and repent."[6] In the fifteenth century
Savonarola found that Florence had a powerless church. In the sixteenth century Pascal found a similar condition in France, and Lati-
mer in Britain, Luther in Germany, Zwingli in Zürich. In the seven-
teenth century the deadness in the churches appalled young George
Fox, founder of the Quakers, as he traveled through Lancashire and
Nottinghamshire. Fox was not an Oxford-trained Englishman, but
he saw all too clearly that there was a lack of "tender" people in the
"steeple-houses"—to use his way of putting it.

I heard of a great meeting to be at Leicester, for a dispute, wherein
Presbyterians, Independents, Baptists, and Common-prayermen were said
to be all concerned. The meeting was in a steeple-house; and thither I was
moved by the Lord to go, and be amongst them. I heard their discourse and
reasonings, some being in pews, and the priest in the pulpit; abundance of
people being gathered together.

At last one woman asked a question out of Peter, What that birth was,
viz., a being born again of incorruptible seed, by the Word of God, that
liveth and abideth for ever? And the priest said to her, "I permit not a
woman to speak in the church"; though he had before given liberty for any
to speak.

Whereupon I was wrapped up, as in a rapture, in the Lord's power; and I stepped up and asked the priest, "Dost thou call this [the steeple-house] a church? Or dost thou call this mixed multitude a church?" But, instead of answering me, he asked me what a church was. I told him, "The church was the pillar and ground of truth, made up of living stones, living members, a spiritual household, which Christ was the head of: but he was not the head of a mixed multitude, or of an old house made up of lime, stones, and wood." This set them all on fire. . . .[7]

Many are calling the similar condition that exists in many of our churches today a "spiritual blackout"—not so much a lack of vision as a loss of power. Bishop Lesslie Newbigin of the Church of South India wrote, "If we would answer the question, 'Where is the Church?' we must ask, 'Where is the Holy Spirit recognizably present with power?'"[8] Samuel M. Shoemaker commented aptly on the bishop's remark: "It would take a theologian with a fine-tooth comb to find the Holy Spirit 'recognizably present with power' in much of our ecclesiastical routine."[9]

But let us not join the mournful chorus that is croaking about the "demise of the church." Let us rather study the problem through a hypothetical life situation. The Reverend John Witherspoon Smith committed his life to Jesus Christ at a Youth for Christ rally at the age of seventeen. At the time, he felt a burning desire to give his life completely to God. "I'll go where You want me to go, dear Lord." So he listened to his elders and they sent him off to school. He completed his training, received ordination, was called to a church pulpit, signed up with the pension plan, found a wife, became a taxpayer, joined the establishment, cut his lawn, and reared a family.

Nothing was wrong with any of it. It was all good. But somewhere along the line Mr. Smith learned by experience that the church is a human institution, made up of people, some of whom are motivated more by personal considerations than by Jesus Power. Among them were those who bore a distinct resemblance to the leaders in the New Testament who preferred the chief seats in the synagogue. Mr. Smith learned that the power game went on in the church as it goes on everywhere, and it was soon evident that he was not the fair-haired boy of his state denominational organization. He tried tailoring his message more to the denomination's liking, but nothing happened. He became disillusioned. In his bitterness of spirit he failed to turn to the Biblical resources God has provided. His people did not stand with him in prayer. Result: his spiritual fuel line became clogged. The Jesus Power that sent him into the ministry was no longer getting through. But he had a nice wife, so he decided to leave the church and take up marriage counseling for a living.

Now let us see what can be learned from this illustration. John Smith discovered that the church is made up of human beings: well and good. We are all human. But then he found churchmen competing against each other for preferment. In an earlier chapter we saw the disciples doing the same thing.[10] Human power apparently seeks to replace Jesus Power as the primary Christian motivator. To that end the church is tempted to package the Gospel with its own self-regarding devices. We Christians offer Jesus Power—plus. Plus what? Plus our hymnbook, our program, our fellowship, the way we do things in our denomination. Is anything wrong with that? Theoretically, no; practically, yes. Instead of pouring power into the convert so he can go out to tell the world about Jesus, we tie him into a pew and drain the power out of him.

When a man walks in the church door, why don't we tell him that all the paraphernalia of the church, including the door itself, are expendable; that none of these things are necessary to get into heaven? Why don't we tell him that he can find all these things in other denominations and even in other religions; that the only distinctive thing we have to offer that can meet his need and get rid of his sins is Jesus Christ, crucified and risen?

Had John Witherspoon Smith put his priorities in order, he would have started preaching the same Gospel that brought him to Christ, and never quit. That Gospel had Jesus Power in it. Had his theological seminary been up to standard it would have set him ablaze for God. Had his denomination been functioning properly it would have built up his morale instead of putting him down. Had his church officers been spiritually alert they would have joined him in taking his problems to God. As for Smith himself, had he been preaching the saving Gospel of Christ he might have been so busy dealing with inquirers that he would not have been aware that he had problems. And he would be in the ministry today.

I have been dealing with a hypothetical case; now let me relate a true story. As a theological student I took a course in the history of missions. In the class I met a young theologue who had just organized a church. Each Monday he reported to us the growth of his congregation, and it made exciting listening, for services were packed morning and evening. At the time I was having trouble getting out a dozen to my student church on Sunday morning, and my Sunday evening youth service consisted of one fourteen-year-old girl. But I knew nothing of Jesus Power, and my friend obviously had something I didn't. I envied him.

Twenty years later I met him again, and by putting two and two together I was able to recall who he was. But now I found him going back in conversation to the past, to the things he used to do. He *had* been in charge of this and that. He then admitted that he was out of the ministry, was teaching psychology in a junior college, and that his wife had left him. My heart went out to him.

"What happened?" I asked.

"I don't know. I guess I ran out of gas," was the reply. *Lord, why were we not able to cast out the demon?*

Jesus Power is the only commodity the church really possesses. There is always a run on Jesus Power, but it is not easy to acquire for the demand exceeds the available supply. The problem is not with the Producer (the Holy Spirit) but with the jobber (the church). People will put up with an awful lot in the church to learn about this power, for they are fed up with the effects of human pride and the raw dealings of the power game. They feel there must be something more to life. When Norman Vincent Peale was a young minister he told his father he was having trouble deciding what to

preach. His father, a minister himself, said to him, "Jesus Christ has
the power to change human lives. Preach that." The church that
proclaims such a message is the church people are looking for. They
will travel miles, cross state, racial, and denominational lines, and dig
deeply into their pockets for such a church. They know instinctively
that it has captured the secret of the New Testament.

Why, then, are such churches in short supply? In pulpit after pulpit
one finds the prayers have become perfunctory and the message has
lost its clout. Unless he goes to an unusual church, the average
middle-aged, middle-class church member is likely to be dis-
couraged by the attendance and confused about his faith. He won-
ders about a lot of things. He hears the clergyman say that because
Jesus was kind, we should be kind. Because Jesus loved the underprivileged and disenfranchised, we should love them. He probably
agrees with that teaching. His difficulty is that at the moment he is
not feeling particularly kind. People are giving him a hard time and
he is feeling sorry for himself rather than for others; and he is not
inclined to change his attitude. He has about all he can take care of
right now. To put it bluntly, he is simply not able to love.

The Apostle Paul warned Timothy against religious types whom
he described as "having a form of godliness but denying the power
thereof."[11] Paul was referring to a particular type of false teacher in
the early church, but I believe his warning has a wider application.
It is easy for a contemporary church to fake a form of godliness,
whatever its theological convictions. We have all worshiped in
churches where the order of service seemed utterly barren and we
could not wait to get outside. When a power failure occurs in a
church, it occurs at this strategic point. The man in the pew cannot
help himself, and the man in the pulpit is not able to communicate
power to him. The form may be present but the content is lacking.
The words may be spoken but they fail to convey reality. When the
next Sunday comes around, the pew is empty.

Having the form of godliness without the power creates an impossible situation. It leads to religious hypocrisy which is the worst type

of all. Ernest T. Campbell has pointed out that many of today's young people have little difficulty in believing that God was in Christ. "What they find hard to accept," he says, "is that Christ is in the church."[12] To implement the teachings of Jesus, one must have the power of Jesus. He gives us the ability to love the unlovable. He trains us to love by faith. He engenders in us a whole new set of attitudes toward people. He drives out the demons of self-love. He makes us empathize with our neighbor. When he comes to dwell in us his power goes to work in us, and that is what the Christian life is all about. The rest is parsley and trimmings.

I do not wish to close this chapter on "the great power failure" without paying my tribute of love to the Christians whose faithful stewardship has kept the doors of our churches open in good times and bad. "The care of all the churches" that Paul wrote about is a very real care. I have taken pains not to comment on theological trends, denominational programs, or social concerns in the various church bodies. My concern is for the life in Christ of the church as a whole. To illustrate the increasingly difficult situation facing most of our large, historic communions, let me describe what takes place each spring.

Earnest ministers and laymen give up a week of their lives to attend their denominational conventions. There they sift through reports of boards and agencies and special commissions. They allocate funds so the church may run smoothly for another fiscal year. They pass resolutions about the plight of the peoples of the world. Because their church is losing ground, they discuss whether they should not merge with another body that is also in trouble, and so eliminate duplication of effort both at home and on the mission field. They look somberly at the latest statistics showing that scores of churches on their rolls have not baptized or received a new member on profession of faith during the past twelve months. They note the declining Sunday school, declining church attendance, declining budget, declining number of missionaries on the field, declining number of new churches, growing number of merging and vacant churches. These are tragic statistics. They sound like the book of Acts in reverse; they even bear a resemblance to the falling off of railroad passenger traffic in North America. The difference is that while the passenger trains have been supplanted by another prime mover, nothing has supplanted the church. Nothing can. The church has the treasure of the Gospel, the pearl of great price that can never be replaced. Nothing is wrong with the church's message and nothing is wrong with Jesus Power. If the church is in trouble the problem must lie elsewhere. But when the week is over the convention adjourns and the delegates go home.

During one hundred years from 1850 to 1950 the churches of North America poured millions of dollars into China. Christian gifts built churches, schools, universities, seminaries, hospitals, orphanages, retreat houses, mission compounds. It was a stupendous investment in real property, an expression of the love of God's people for their fellow men. Today it is gone, every square foot of it. The government of the People's Republic has appropriated the physical equipment and is using it for storing rice and other things. What is left of the church in China? Stories are coming through telling of pockets of vitality here and there. People are meeting in homes. Bibles are treasured and passed from hand to hand. Christians are living in the Spirit, sharing the blessings of the Grace of God despite the disapproval of the authorities. The church is not dying, it is going on Jesus Power. *And that was all the church had to begin with!*

Statistics in America show a power failure in the church, but not a failure of Jesus Power. Perhaps it is not too late to learn that George Fox's "steeple-houses" and other church real estate are not as essential as we thought. Perhaps our young people have already absorbed that lesson. We shall see.

Chapter 10

The Jesus People

The street people share everything they have with everybody and make no apologies about it. They just say,
"Here, have some cheese." Or, "Have some bread." Or
whatever. And the same thing happens after they have
found Jesus Christ. When they talk with you they very
naturally say, "I want you to meet Jesus Christ. He's
where it's at. He'll give you the peace you're after."[1]
                                    —DUANE C. PEDERSON

As a young city editor I would strike out the name "Jesus" whenever
it appeared in news copy that came across my desk. I was merely
following my training; in those days newspapermen considered religious terminology outside the realm of ordinary news coverage.
Christ was seldom referred to in the public meetings I reported.
Businessmen would avoid mentioning the name of God and would
speak instead of "Christianity," "churches," or "religion." When I
entered theological seminary in 1940 I discovered that Christ was
not faring much better in the textbooks. The New Testament scholars whom we studied regarded Jesus as a blown-up savior figure, a
kind of religious folk hero around whom his early followers had
built a series of legends. The critical task of the experts, it seemed,
was to peel away the supernatural and mythological encrustation and
so get down to the "real Jesus." The trouble was, no one agreed on
just who the real Jesus was. Some thought of him as a romantic
itinerant carpenter, others as a deluded prophet of the end of the
world, still others as a political revolutionary. By the time we stu-

dents had waded through these patronizing theories, it was hard to muster much devotion toward Jesus in the twenty minutes of chapel.

Sometimes on a clear morning I can hear the laughter in heaven. I believe God deliberately raised up the Jesus Movement to confound all those who have been embarrassed to talk about Jesus; who found his name sticking in their throats; who avoided direct reference to him by substituting the word "religion." It seems the desert finally got so dry the heavenly Father had to soak it with a cloudburst. So it happened that during the mid-sixties, at the very moment when the "God-is-dead" theologians were projecting their theories, Jesus Power began to move in some young hearts. Within a few years flowers were blooming in the wasteland. Now we see and hear his name everywhere: Jesus! Jesus! Jesus!

To say that the denigrators of the Person of Jesus Christ have been astonished is to put it mildly. Most of them have clung to their views, but they have been forced to recognize that the traditional Christian position is more solidly entrenched than they thought. Here and there some concessions are being made; it is being suggested that to reduce Jesus to the level of a frustrated religious teacher or a misguided "superstar" may be to draw conclusions too narrow to account for all the evidence.

Further, some of the young people are saying they will not hear of it. When some lectures were given in a prominent church on the West Coast, a delegation of the Jesus People took over the microphone at the close and told the packed audience that the speaker had missed his opportunity; that what was needed in today's world was a supernatural, transcendent God of power. They then proceeded to give their personal testimonies, sharing what Jesus Christ had done for them. They were greeted with a standing ovation—and why not? Who is not eager to find power for his life?

At their invitation I went out with the Jesus People. I sat with them on the grass and knelt with them on the linoleum and the concrete. I clapped the beat until my hands nearly fell off. I sang "Maranatha," "We Are One in the Spirit," "Put Your Hand in the Hand of the

Man of Galilee," and "Amazing Grace." Even while I puzzled over their weird cartoons, I obediently put on their Jesus buttons. I held up my index finger and shouted, "One way!" I shook hands in odd grips, joined in "spell yells" for Jesus, slapped stickers on my brief-case and telephone, and even let my hair grow out a bit.

Not that I minded it all; and the young people, it must be said, were most gracious. They did not mention that I was over thirty by a good bit. They snubbed neither me nor my generation. They loved us, asked us questions, rapped with us, and witnessed to us. It's so obvious that our buttoned-down era is on its way into history and that the gap between the generations is very real. Yet I felt more at home among today's Jesus People than in the tired atmosphere of many a dwindling middle-aged, middle-class congregation.

The difference is Jesus, of course, for he is the Life-bringer. He has infused some of our young people with a zeal I never expected to see again in this century. My own faith being not much larger than a mustard seed, I had thought that the classic days of revival were over. Even while we prayed for God to send a revival to our churches, I doubted that it would come. I had read books on the subject and was convinced that the last real breath of the Spirit—apart from planned evangelistic campaigns and sporadic manifesta-tions at Christian colleges—was observed on the island of Lewis in the Outer Hebrides in the year 1950, on the very fringes of com-munication. It seemed to me that the electronic invasion—television—had killed any possibilities of spontaneous spiritual awakening on a large scale in our time. "How unsearchable are his judgments, and his ways past finding out!"[2]

What a revelation it has been to see the really significant detona-tion of Jesus Power in our day taking place not in some remote, untelevised corner of the planet; not in the kraals of Zululand or the thatched community houses of the Solomon Islands; but right here at home! The Spirit of God is moving among youth in our great Western cities, at our institutions of learning, on our beaches. Start-ing on the West Coast of America, the tide of interest has moved eastward and has been carried by young people across the Atlantic. European Christian leaders appear fascinated by it. Billy Graham told the press in Amsterdam that it was the greatest contemporary movement in America. The fact that it originated among youth is in its favor: all the significant movements of the church from the time of the twelve disciples have been staffed by young personnel. To visit a "campus church" and observe it in action is to realize that God has set his seal on the work. The waters are running too deep to be temporary.

The Jesus Movement, or Jesus Revolution, as it is sometimes called, is closely linked to the new drug culture that has staggered and demoralized our sophisticated Western youth. To say that the Jesus Revolution was born out of the drug crisis would be wrong, for it is obviously a movement born of God. But thousands of our young people have been involved—by their own testimony—with demons and supernaturally evil forces in their drug "trips." Christopher Pike, the surviving son of the late Bishop James Pike and a member of the Jesus Movement, assured me that no one can take LSD pills for any length of time without encountering demons.[3] The horror of these experiences has caused some young people to turn to the only power they knew who could help them: Jesus Christ, who drove demons out of people in his lifetime and made an open show of them in his death.[4] It's hardly surprising that the Jesus Movement has a high Christology!

As the popularity of hallucinogenic drugs began to rise in California in 1966 and 1967, and spread to other parts of the nation and the world, so the Jesus Movement is traveling in the same direction. It is a case of God making the wrath of man to praise him.[5] Jesus People have their faddish aspects; commercializers and exploiters are finding them a good thing; extremists are hiving off and forming intolerant factions that hurt the witness of the young people; and there are hypocrites here as everywhere. Some youths claim to be "into Jesus" while they continue to live at the moral level of street people. In spite of these and other drawbacks, the Jesus Movement has become one of the most hopeful signs of spiritual life in the churches of the Western world during the seventies. Such a development is all the more striking as the movement began with only the most tenuous of links with the organized church.

The rootless young people who formed communes and Bible study groups and constituted the original Jesus People compose but a small segment of the Christian youth population of North America today. Yet their influence has been enormous. They are the pacesetters, fashion stylers, and innovators. They have written much of the music that Christian youth is now singing. They have developed fresh ideas in youth evangelism. The more conventional, churchgoing youth are taking their cues from what is happening among their less inhibited peers. It seems certain that in time the lines of distinction will be blurred and that the Jesus Movement will become part and parcel of church life. Edward E. Plowman, in his study of the movement, describes a youth revival that began in a Methodist church in Greensburg, Kentucky and moved to the high-school campus:

Young people wept at the altar, embraced and prayed for each other. They held rallies at the high school, organized lunchtime prayer groups, witnessed in the halls and outside. Long-haired boozers and dopers received Christ. Parents and teachers told me they could hardly believe the dramatic change of attitude in some youths. Clusters of non-Christians around high school spoke incredulously of their friends' changed lives and of the joy they sensed on the campus. Enemies of long standing untangled the discord of years in one unforgettable moment of forgiveness and outpoured Christian love.[6]

A spate of books has appeared about the Jesus Revolution and more are coming. I have no gift of prophecy, but I will ask the question that many are asking: Do we have in the Jesus Movement an authentic demonstration of supernatural power such as the Holy Spirit has used in the past to mark his Presence in his church? My conclusions lead me to respond on the favorable side. I rest my opinion not on the prayer life of the young people, though there is prayer; not on their moral and ethical standards, though they are to be commended for the testimony of their lives; and not on their study of the Word of God, though their devotion to Scripture is impressive. The one criterion above all else that has convinced me of the genuineness and authority of the Jesus People is their evidence of love.

The whole atmosphere around these young people is bathed in love; one cannot get away from it. Painted sweat shirts, buttons, bumper stickers, posters, tabloids, guitars, drums, microphones, are all devoted to telling the old story of Jesus' love in a novel, contemporaneous, and exuberant way. Of the Jesus People, as of few Christians since Pentecost, it could be said that they could be taken for drunk at nine o'clock in the morning.[7] They radiate a quiet joy such as the early Franciscans knew. Their music reflects a holy hilarity. They have offered the first inducement in years to make me want to be young again. Love, joy, and peace are the best-known fruits of the Spirit, and the Jesus Revolution has them all.

Love is never irresponsible, and I have noted a quiet social passion in the Jesus People that marks them as children of the new generation. They make no distinctions based on origin or skin color; like the Apostle Paul, they hold that God is no respecter of persons. They do not discriminate against people because of age, sex, race, or status. They have broken down the Protestant-Catholic and Christian-Jewish barriers. Their love is uninhibited by the canons that divided their parents and grandparents. They take the responsibility of sharing the Gospel seriously; one finds them everywhere the young people are gathering today. At the music festivals, on the beaches, in the parks, they may be seen distributing literature and gently making their testimony. It is a beautiful thing to watch. These people know how to communicate love, and they are winning thousands of their colleagues to Christ.

Dr. Edward V. Hill, pastor of one of the great black churches of America, Mt. Zion Missionary Baptist Church of Watts in the inner city of Los Angeles, once said, "Some laymen have thought that when no one accepted Christ, the pastor was losing his power. Don't you know that shepherds do not have sheep? *Sheep have sheep.* Every saved soul is saved to help save others."[8]

When one of these young people is converted to Jesus Christ, he may or may not start attending a church, but he is pretty certain to start working among his former friends in the drug culture, or witchcraft, or Satan worship, or the sex treadmill, seeking to rescue them from their self-destructive traps and to bring them into the glorious light of human freedom. While many churches continue their irrelevant ministries to the saved and bored, these youths, often startling in appearance, are carrying out the Great Commission in the spirit of C. T. Studd, who wrote:

> Some wish to live within the sound
> Of church or chapel bell,
> I want to run a rescue shop
> Within a yard of hell.[9]

Right now there is as much power in evidence in the Jesus Movement as in any other aspect of church life: not political power, not ecclesiastical power, but spiritual vitality. The question persists: will this power move from the music festivals and parades and rallies and singouts and Bible houses and retreats and ranches into the local church on the corner? Will the "Right on's" be mixed with the "Amens"? Sad stories are being related by ex-street people about the reception they have received in some churches. When the power has been shut off at the church's meter box, it is easy to mistake aesthetics for ethics and culture habits for Christian living. Scripture says nothing about the superiority of the wind instrument (the organ) to the stringed instrument (the guitar), but older Christians assume it, as they assume short hair and Sunday suits.

In spite of its conservative ways, its callousness, and its power outage, God has not abandoned the local church. Ours is not the first age in which congregations needed reviving. My prayer is that before the present "Jesus generation" is disillusioned and turned off completely, the pastors and leaders of our churches will have the grace, the wisdom, and the humility to say to these Christian young people, "Please come into our churches and bring your love. Come as you are. We need you. We're not opposed to the Jesus Movement. We just want to get in on it!"

Chapter 11

The Word of Power

I get hungry for the Word the way I get hungry for a
piece of beefsteak.[1]

—A DAY LABORER NAMED STEVE

LLOYD C. Douglas once wrote a novel, *Magnificent Obsession*, in
which an artist showed a friend a single page of the Bible that was
said to carry a "mysterious potentiality." According to the artist, it
gave "the rules for getting whatever you want, and doing whatever
you wish to do, and being whatever you would like to be." The artist
said he had heard the words read in a church service and they had
stirred him profoundly. He had hurried home and looked up the
passage in his own Bible. As he later told his friend, "There it was
—in black and white—the exact process for achieving power . . ."[2]

The novelist did not divulge which page it was, and he did not
need to. He was saying in his own way that the Bible is a book of
power.

People approach the Bible in hundreds of different ways. Some
choose to adore the book without so much as opening it. For such,
Holy Scripture is little more than a fetish to be worshiped. Others
appear to hold it in some respect ("I'll swear on a stack of Bibles")
but keep as far away from it as possible lest it interfere with their
life-style. Others attribute magical qualities to the Book although it
contains not one word of magic or sorcery. Others actively pervert
the Bible's use: Satanists and occultists are using it today in varied
forms of demon worship. For others the Bible is a human artifact,
a unique archaeological document. They examine it with scientific

care and write volumes explaining how it came to be written and compiled, how its canon was formed, how it relates to other ancient literature, how its complex passages should be interpreted, and so on. Still others treat the Bible as a literary masterpiece to be studied for its contribution to the humanities. And some people fragment the Bible for their special interests, selecting those parts that suit their purposes and rejecting or ignoring the rest.

All of these approaches have their respective advocates and defenders, but we must leave them, for our study is aimed at another target. We are seeking to discover the divine extra, the "mysterious potentiality" that is locked up in the Bible, and to see whether it is accessible to men. Christianity claims that the Bible is different from all other literature, sacred or secular. What is that difference? Is it elevation of moral tone, brilliance of thought, beauty of language, or veracity of information? Not entirely, for most of these are differences of degree, and the Bible's unrivaled status as a power source is a difference in kind.

Again and again in the pages of the Old and New Testaments the Bible is described as the Word of God. This is the same Word by which the heavens were made[3] and which was given to the Israelites at Mount Sinai.[4] It is the Word which was in the beginning with God, and which became flesh in Jesus Christ.[5] It is called the Book of the Lord, the Book of the Law, the Good Word of God, the Holy Scriptures, the Law of the Lord, the Oracles of God, the Scriptures of Truth, the Sword of the Spirit, the Word of Christ, the Word of Life, and the Word of Truth.[6] More important for our immediate consideration, it is called the Word of his [God's] Power.[7]

The supreme difference between the Bible and other writings of whatever kind, in my opinion, is that these sixty-six books are in fact the Word of God's Power. They possess a supernatural character because they are inspired by God; that is to say, God breathed through them and used them to reveal himself to men. When J. B. Phillips was translating the New Testament he wrote that he "felt rather like an electrician rewiring an ancient house without being able to 'turn the mains off.' "[8] About no other book could that be written, because no other book achieves that effect.

However, the supernatural power in the Bible is not readily evident to men. It has to be believed to be experienced. To respect the Bible, to worship it, to examine it, to dissect it, to regard it as a cultural tool is not enough. Only one way leads to the Bible's inner strength. When the Spirit of Power has enlightened the mind of the reader, the Word of Power becomes real.

Suppose we do assume that the Bible is nothing more than a human document like *Hamlet* or the *Origin of Species.* Immediately every article of Christian faith is relegated to the rubble pile of history. Israel's God is dead; Christ is a mere "superstar"; the Spirit is vapor; the sacraments are a waste; the church is a country club; the grave is the end. Only the doctrine of original sin remains intact. However, even under such conditions we cannot assume that the Bible is powerless. God can speak through his Word even in an atmosphere of unbelief. Men have actually been converted listening to God's Word being read in derision. "Faith cometh by hearing, and hearing by the word of God."[9] And when we take up the Scriptures in faith as God's revelation, then we begin really to *know* the Bible's power. When we recognize that in the Old and New Testaments men are writing truth as God speaks to them, switches are thrown and the dynamos of the Spirit begin to hum.

What does it mean to say the Bible is "inspired"? John R. W. Stott told the Inter-Varsity Student Missionary Convention at Urbana, Illinois:

Our view of Scripture is derived from Christ's view of Scripture, just as our view of discipleship, of heaven and hell, of the Christian life, and of everything else, is derived from Jesus Christ. Any question about the inspiration of Scripture and its authority therefore resolves itself to: What did Jesus Christ teach about these points? We would say without any doubt that he gave reverent assent to the authority and inspiration of the Old Testament. He regarded the words of the Old Testament writings as being the words of God. He submitted to them in his own life. He accepted their statements and sought to apply their principles. He regarded Scripture as the great arbiter in dispute. We find in the New Testament that he invested the apostles with authority to teach in his name. He said that the Holy Spirit would lead them into all truth, would bring to their remembrance what he had spoken to them, and would show them things to come. He evidently expected that in the providence of God there would be others to interpret, expound and bear witness to the revelation given in himself, just as prophets were raised up by God to bear witness to what he did in Old Testament days. In sum, the authority of Scripture is due to the inspiration of Scripture. The Old and New Testaments are authoritative in our lives because they are in fact inspired.[10]

Jesus Power began to flow in my life when I concluded, after fourteen years of intellectual struggle, that I was not an authority on the Bible. Instead, the Bible was an authority on me. I continued (and continue) to recognize the presence of immense difficulties in the sacred text. I had no bishop to allegorize my stubborn passages for me as Ambrose did for Augustine.[11] My intelligence was permanently insulted; I had to act on naked faith. If Scripture said that "the iron did swim,"[12] I accepted that it did in fact float—though the precise arrangement of the molecules in that axhead was something I was not prepared to diagram.

My new attitude toward the Holy Scripture failed to clear up the seeming contradictions and discontinuities; if anything it increased them. No longer could I naturalize the miracles by nattering on about "optical illusions." If Jesus diagnosed an illness as demon possession I could not pass it off as epilepsy. Yet I found that the heavenly Father did not object at all to my ignorance or inability to understand the text; nor did he complain when I told him that it was his problem and he could solve it. He seemed willing enough for me to defer the difficult passages for later enlightenment and explanation. He did not even require, now that I had dropped the role of "higher critic," that I become a defender of his Word. Nowhere in the Bible have I been able to find that we must stand up for the Scriptures. "Defend the Bible?" Spurgeon once exclaimed. "I would as soon defend a lion." Paul said he was set for the defense of the Gospel,[13] and Jude bade us contend for the faith,[14] but evidently the Bible itself needs no human guardians.

Where did we get the idea that the Bible is some kind of fragile archive that needs our plastic-cover protection lest it be corroded by pollutants? The Bible is a rapier of steel, to be seized and used against the principalities and powers of darkness. It is a weapon, not a book. It is a tool for the building of mature Christians. The Bible is something you do things with. It is for use. That is to say, it is a book of action, written by active people for active people. It is a book of power. It was never intended to be bound in morocco and hidden on shelves. It is neither a glorified reference work nor a textbook of systematic theology. God apparently does not object to scholars immersing themselves in Biblical interpretation, but the Bible was not written for scholars; and when scholars claim to be authorities on the text apart from the inspiration and power of the Holy Spirit, they might better become Egyptologists. God, said Pascal, is the God of Abraham, Isaac, and Jacob—not the God of savants and philosophers.[15]

What does it mean to say that the Bible is inspired? Abraham Kuyper, lifelong Bible student and one-time prime minister of the Netherlands, expressed it this way.

Inspiration is the name of that all-comprehensive operation of the Holy Spirit whereby he has bestowed on the church a complete and infallible Scripture. We call this operation all-comprehensive for it was organic, not mechanical. . . . The confession of inspiration does not exclude ordinary numbering, collecting of documents, sifting, and recording. It recognizes all these matters which are plainly discernible in Scripture. Style, diction, repetitions, all retain their value. But it must be insisted that the Scripture as a whole, as finally presented to the church, owes its existence to the Holy Spirit as to content, selection, and arrangement of documents, structure, and even words. The men employed in this work were consciously or unconsciously so controlled and directed by the Spirit, in all their thinking, selecting, sifting, choice of words, and writing, that their final product, delivered to posterity, possessed a warrant of divine and absolute authority.[16]

Kuyper points out that the stumbling blocks in Scripture require the exercise of faith beyond the intellectual grasp; and so it has proved for me. Just as I have found love to be the key to the power of the Spirit, so I have found faith to be the key to the power of the Word; and since it is one and the same power, both keys are essential. Yet it cannot be assumed that once faith in God is awakened, power automatically flows. Because a person has accepted the plenary inspiration and authority of Scripture, he is not thereby necessarily supernaturally empowered. We can proclaim our undying devotion to the truth of the Bible and still discover that the demon has stayed in the child, right where he was. After all, why not? The demons also believe the Bible. A positive stance toward the original documents of the faith is no guarantee of Jesus Power.

The power comes after a man has been depowered. Jesus told his disciples that when the Paraclete came, he would convict the world concerning sin and righteousness and judgment.[17] Paul wrote to Timothy that the purpose of inspired Scripture was to teach, to reprove, to correct, and to discipline.[18] Until there is repentance there can be no true faith and there can be no supernatural power. When the Scriptures take hold of a man and shake him to his foundation and empty him of his pride and his lust for human power, he then becomes a candidate for Jesus Power.

After the way has been cleared and the living water is flowing between the banks, the Bible comes into its own. It becomes a divine instrument for piercing the hearts and consciences of men and women as it is opened, and quoted, and studied, and preached, and shared. No other book does so, because no other book is God's book in the sense that the Bible is. Many centuries before Christ the prophet Isaiah quoted his Lord as saying, "My word . . . shall not return unto me void, but it shall accomplish that which I please, and it shall prosper in the thing whereto I sent it."[19]

Which version of the Bible is the easiest for God to work with? For several years after the new translations of the English Bible began to appear, I doubted whether they could be used effectively in evangelism. My faith was scotch-taped to the India pages of the King James Version. It took the young people of the Jesus Movement really to convince me that God is unlimited in the use he makes of language. Truth cannot operate through error; inaccurate translations are never acceptable; but many good and reliable versions are available today.

The Bible is not the easiest book to read and understand. Even with the Holy Spirit's clarifying insight, the ancient truth cannot always be grasped by the average reader. Certainly without such insight the text—indeed, the very purpose—of the Biblical writings is lost in the musty corridors of a strange language. I recall once investigating an abandoned mission at Fortymile, on the Yukon Rive near the Canadian-Alaskan border. Finding a Bible, I took it back to my rowboat and read it as my partner and I drifted downriver. What I read made no sense to me beyond giving me a vague guilt feeling, for I was not a Christian at the time. My confusion exceeded that of the Ethiopian eunuch.[20] I could not understand why some words were italicized in the text, apparently without reason. Never in a thousand years would I have guessed that those words did not appear in the original Greek!

Even had I known about the italicized words, I would still have found the Bible a mystery. Men can provide information and knowledge, but only God provides wisdom. Only Christ can open the Scriptures to us and make our hearts burn within us. As Paul B. Smith says,

If we want to understand the Bible we must be acquainted with the Divine Author of the Bible. We need that personal knowledge of God that comes when a man trusts Jesus Christ as his Savior, enters into the experience of the new birth and becomes a member of the family of God. When this happens we are given the spiritual eyesight that is essential to a study of the Scriptures.[21]

After I became bogged down trying to read the Bible I pitched it overboard. Many another man and woman has done the same. They have tried to struggle through a book or two and have given it up as hopeless—and for a very good reason.

The Bible is not simply words on a page, it is spiritual food provided by God to nourish the spiritual life of a believer. Just as the human body needs daily food and exercise, so the human soul needs the nutrition provided by God's Word. Yet here the analogy ends; for the soul of man does not respond to the pangs of hunger as his body does. The more spiritual food we get, the more we want; and the less we get, the less we seem to want. The world today is filled with people walking around, carrying powerful physiques and sickly, shrunken souls. Only one food will restore health to the inner man and make him powerful for God; that is the manna of God's Word.[22]

Chapter 12

Press-Box Theology

God, the God I love and worship, reigns in sorrow on the Tree,
Broken, bleeding, but unconquered, very God of God to me. . . .
On my knees I fall and worship that great Cross that shines above,
For the very God of Heaven is not Power, but Power of Love.[1]
—G. A. STUDDERT-KENNEDY (1883–1929)

THE business of the church, says Ray Stedman in his fine study of
Body Life,[2] is primarily not to evangelize the world, but to build
persons conformable to the image of Jesus Christ. Building people,
like building skyscrapers, takes power. Construction work is heavy
work. The pyramids of Egypt were built by human power, thousands
of slaves dragging and rolling the massive blocks into position.
Modern office centers are built by mechanical power, compressors,
electric drills, giant cranes. Christians are built by Jesus Power,
which changes life direction and motivates to new goals. To carry
the analogy farther, the church is the powerhouse from which feeder
lines go out to the service units. Back of the powerhouse are the
viaducts and watersheds of the Holy Spirit.

Metaphors have their uses. The New Testament speaks of the
church as the "body of Christ" and again as the "bride of Christ,"
to instruct Christians in their relationship to their Lord and to each
other. Metaphors, however, are not intended to close our eyes to the
nature of the church or to its mission. The church is not primarily
a powerhouse, a holy temple, a sacred institution, a divinely ap-
pointed hierarchy, a mystical body, an invisible choir, a place of
proclamation, a mission outstation, a vehicle for dispensing the sacra-

ments, a bearer of apostolic tradition, a cloud of witnesses, or a heavenly mystery. All these marks of the church, important as they are, are overshadowed by the New Testament teaching that the church is primarily a called-out assembly of *people*. No matter how many attributes we attach to it, the *ek-klesia* is still made up of flesh-and-blood human beings. Dr. Carl Wisløff of Oslo, in words that are reminiscent of George Fox,[3] made the point to the European Congress on Evangelism in Amsterdam in 1971.

The *ekklesia* of God is no house built of brick or wood, nor is it an institution. It stands for the people of God. In the New Testament the church is a fellowship of people. The church is not "something," but "some." It is not a building that believers and unbelievers inhabit [which is what George Fox, in the earlier reference, meant by a "mixed multitude"]. The church is a building that is built up of believers as living stones. The walls do not enclose the faithful; rather the faithful are the walls.

Since the church is a fellowship of believers, and since this fellowship is created by the one true Gospel, it follows that the church is *one*. The opposite of the one church is not many churches, but the false church, the pseudochurch.[4]

If Dr. Stedman's thesis is correct, the church is far more than a powerhouse, a warehouse, or any other kind of stable structure; it is a freeway for the conveying of construction materials with which to build men. God, for reasons known only to himself, has chosen to use the church. He doesn't need the church, but he has created it, summoned it, and ordained it for its task. What's more, he intends to make maximum use of it wherever it doesn't set up roadblocks to hinder his work.

Before we can continue our discussion of Jesus Power, we shall have to deal with the question of the roadblocks. What are they? How can they be dealt with? The New Testament mentions many of them: lack of private and corporate prayer; inattention to the Word of God; unwillingness to witness to the saving power of Christ; immorality among church members; a breakdown in the spiritual life of the church's leadership; quarrelsome factions; a failure to communicate the Gospel clearly; weak administration of the church's affairs; unconcern for the needy; pride; racism; withholding of what belongs to God; lack of evangelistic zeal; opaque missionary vision; and so on. Any one of these afflictions has the effect of blocking the circulation of spiritual traffic.

Equipment may be necessary to remove a roadblock. Skill and training will help the church fulfill its commission; but where hindrances such as immorality, pride, and callousness impede the way, knowledge alone won't do the job. The church has plenty of know-how, what it needs is "can-do." Maintenance men are required who will spot the cause of the obstruction and work at it until the way is clear. The call is not just for expertise but for something far more important.

Every manager of an organization knows the value of morale and seeks to maintain it one way or another. The church is the only human institution whose morale is founded entirely and unabashedly on love. For two thousand years it has proved the truth of its message of love by the way it has lived. When we look at the church's record we find that love = morale = spiritual power. On the other hand, no love = low morale = no power. That is because the church's charter is John 3:16, "God loved the world so much that he gave his only Son so that anyone who believes in him shall not perish but have eternal life."[5] Jesus added an amendment to the charter for our sakes. He said, "By this all men will know that you are my disciples, if you have love for one another."[6] God's power, as Studdert Kennedy says, is the power of love. The Holy Spirit draws by love. Christians are saved by love. As they are built into the image of Christ, love provides the ready-mix. When a breakdown occurs in the life of the church, the cause might be anything —doctrinal error, carnal sin, someone playing the power game, or something else—but whatever the cause, the breakdown is usually accompanied by a failure of love.

After studying the tremendous emphasis placed on love by the

"Jesus Movement" in our day, I would like to put forward a tentative press-box theology. By "press-box" I mean that these ideas did not come out of a classroom or a library (although I owe a great deal to both). They have come out of an open Bible in the press boxes of about sixty stadiums around the world. Here for fourteen years my colleagues and I have been watching the Holy Spirit working in the hearts of men and women during the Billy Graham crusades.

Press-box theology is quite simple: it is love in action. Co-workers on the Graham team tell me they never get tired of going to crusades because so much love is expressed in them, and who can have too much of love? There is love between man and God, between believer and believer, and between inquirer and counselor. That is what the Gospel of Jesus Christ is all about—love. Not sophistication, not urbanity, not artificiality or insensitivity, but love. And how do you get love? From a warm heart. And how does a heart become warm? It catches fire. When John the Baptist said, "I baptize you with water, but he who is mightier than I . . . will baptize you with the Holy Spirit and with fire,"[7] he was talking about the fire of love. When the tongues of flame appeared at Pentecost, and the Holy Spirit's presence was felt and known, it was a baptism of love that God poured out on the whole church. Wrote Samuel Chadwick:

Fire is the chosen symbol of heaven for moral passion. God is love; God is fire. The two are one. The Holy Spirit baptizes in fire. Spirit-filled souls are ablaze for God. They love with a love that glows. They believe with a faith that kindles. They serve with a devotion that consumes. They hate sin with a fierceness that burns. They rejoice with a joy that radiates. Love is perfected in the fire of God.[8]

So here is the gist of a "press-box theology": the baptism of the Spirit is a baptism of love, the filling of the Spirit is a filling of love, the power of the Spirit is the power of love. God's transcendent love becomes incarnate in human flesh in our own day and moves out where the action is.

Jesus Power is love power, and love power is fire power, and it works. But note an important fact: it works only in individuals, never in groups.

From our seats in the press box it is easy to observe that "mass evangelism" and "mass conversion" are artificial terms. Whatever really happens in the stadium during the service happens in the hearts of individuals. God's love is personal. Jesus Power is personal. Interestingly, Adolf Berle's study of "power" corroborates this view.[9] Power, he says, is "invariably personal. However attained, it can be exercised only by the decision and act of an individual. There is no such thing as 'class power,' 'elite power,' or 'group power,' though classes, elites, and groups may assist processes of organization by which power is lodged in individuals." The analogy holds true in the spiritual realm. Jesus Power cannot be sprayed over a stadium crowd or over a church congregation by a wave of the hand. The church is, in fact, simply an organization by which Jesus Power is lodged in individuals.

The Marxists recognize the inadequacy of mass propaganda as a means of changing people's basic attitudes. Their leaders from Lenin to Mao have insisted that the "revolution" is a success only when it has been accepted by individuals. In depression days when Soviet theory was attracting many leading European and American intellectuals, it was not uncommon for a young idealist to seek membership in the Communist Party and to give as his reason the wistful hope that the social ills of all men could be cured. The Party cadres took a poor view of such altruism. They insisted, "You will never make a good Communist until you want it for *yourself.*"

Our Lord was not unaware of the self-interest motive; he taught, "You shall love your neighbor as your own self."[10] But he also stipulated another kind of love: he demanded that the self be given to him! Robert Boyd Munger says, "I had to learn that the Lord wanted me before he wanted my service." According to our press-box theology, the baptism of love means that the self has quit making self-regard its be-all and end-all. Love forgets itself and goes out and makes friends. When Jesus Power is coming through we drop the artificial posture, the effort to "protect the image," and stay with love. We are crucified with Christ; what we have now is Christ living in us.[11]

What would happen if evangelical Christians were to take Galatians 2:20 seriously and begin letting Christ love through us? Perhaps the first step would be to admit that we have not been doing it. I suggest the following kind of statement adopted by the churches would clear the decks for action:

We of the evangelical community would like to confess that we have not loved everybody as we should have done.

We have placed emphasis on sound doctrine, and rightly, for there is no compromise between truth and error. But we have not always proclaimed that truth in a loving manner.

We have warned about judgment, because we are aware with every passing hour that our world is on a collision course bound for destruction. Yet our admonitions have not always been watered with the tears of genuine affection.

We have insisted to people that they must be born again, but our attitudes toward them have not always made it seem that being born again is such a wonderful thing after all.

We have talked about hell but we have not done it with broken hearts.

We have made much of the fact that Jesus went among the publicans and sinners, but we have made no bones about preferring our own company.

We have tried to draw people into the Kingdom of God by a plethora of words instead of by love, and have wondered why we have not had more success.

We have told today's young people that they needed to be saved, and after they were saved we have many times acted toward them as if we did not want them saved after all; as if all we really wanted was for them to get their hair cut or something equally irrelevant.

We have prided ourselves on being Good Samaritans to the world's unfortunate, when the unfortunates themselves often must have felt that we were busy-busy priests and Levites passing by on the other side.

We have walked away from too many problems in order to preach the

Bible, only to ignore those parts of the Bible that deal with those same specific problems.

We have tried to convey the impression on occasion that we are better than the rest of the people, instead of admitting with Paul that we are the chief of sinners.

We have testified about our being justified by Grace alone, but have sometimes subtly managed to infer that this was some kind of achievement on our part.

We have fought and clawed like tomcats over the precious Gospel of love.

Under the circumstances we would like to mend our fences. We would like to say to the human race that we have behaved rather badly toward some of our neighbors. We have done things we wish we hadn't, and have neglected things we wish we had taken care of.

We ask forgiveness.[12]

Any such confession should make it clear that our failings are not the failings of the Lord Jesus Christ; that while we may deny him, he cannot deny himself. Salvation through his blood is still rich and free. Of Christ it can be said, in Marshall McLuhan's phrase, that "the medium is the message." He is the way, the truth, and the life, and no answer will be found to the problems of this bandaged and bleeding world apart from his love. He is the key to love, just as he is the key to power.

Chapter 13

The Power That Revives

Victory in service is to be expected from supernaturally
born men and women who are supernaturally delivered,
supernaturally sustained and supernaturally directed. We
are thus supernaturally created for a supernatural work
which is supernaturally prepared and is to be supernaturally performed.[1]

—LEONARD L. LEGTERS (1873–1940)

MANY prophets in our midst are predicting imminent doom for the
human race. I have even heard of a man carrying a sandwich board
in New York's Times Square that read: BEWARE. THE WORLD WILL
NOT COME TO AN END! The Christian faith warns of a coming
judgment, but it does not share the disenchantment and disillusion-
ment that are so popular today, particularly among the young. The
Bible never succumbs to a philosophy of despair. Instead it teaches
us to look ahead to the time when Jesus Christ will return and
establish his Kingdom.

Shortly before his death Dr. Mordecai Ham, the evangelist, paid
a visit to San Francisco where Billy Graham was holding a crusade.
I was in the Cow Palace the night Dr. Ham was introduced as the
man who had led Graham to Christ during a tent campaign in
Charlotte, North Carolina twenty-two years earlier. I heard him tell
the crowd of sixteen thousand people, "Every day I pick up my
newspaper to see what man has been doing. Then I pick up my Bible
to see what God is going to do."

I have thought of that many times. Just what is God going to do?

He will judge the world, that is certain; and Scripture is also clear
about the personal return of the Lord Jesus Christ in clouds of glory.
Yet Jesus intimates that a worldwide revival of faith may take place
before the end of history. Matthew records him as saying, "The glad
tidings of the kingdom of God shall be proclaimed in all the habita-
ble earth [*oikoumene*] for a testimony to all the nations; and then the
end shall come."² If the promise of the Second Advent gives me
hope for the future, the promise of spiritual awakening gets me
positively excited.

Dr. Ham was right. We read our newspapers and news magazines,
we listen to the radio, we watch the newscasts on television, and an
overpowering feeling of *angst* or dread comes through, not just from
the communications people but from everywhere. Each day's report
brings the same dreary information about domestic turmoil, the
escalation of crime, the breakdown of essential services, the waning
confidence of people in their leadership, the sagging influence of the
democracies, the rise of demagoguery and dictatorship, the generation gap, the outbreak of new wars, the shifting balance of power
in the United Nations, increasing anti-Americanism, inflation, the
menace of Communist attack from space satellites. "One can either
go on listening to the news—and of course the news is always bad,
even when it sounds good," Aldous Huxley once said. Or alterna-
tively one can make up one's mind to listen to something else."³

The Bible has that "something else." It teaches that the more sin
abounds in the world, the more Grace will abound to the glory of
God.⁴ What is Grace? Grace is mercy, favor, forgiveness, wisdom,
magnanimity, blessing—and power. It is the power of God at work
in the hearts of men. If our interpretation of Scripture is correct, God
intends to release the power of his Grace into men and women and
young people in every part of the world where he has prepared
hearts to receive his Holy Spirit. On all six continents, in the Arctic
and the Antarctic and on the islands of the sea, people will find
salvation. They will be clothed in the righteousness of Christ and will
be filled with Jesus Power. The church of God will be renewed.

Here is the formula God gave to Solomon three thousand years ago: "If my people who are called by my name humble themselves, and pray and seek my face, and turn from their wicked ways, then I will hear from heaven, and will forgive their sin and heal their land." To the prophet Joel came the Word of the Lord: "I will pour out my spirit upon all flesh; and your sons and your daughters shall prophesy, your old men shall dream dreams, your young men shall see visions. . . ." [5]

Revivals have occurred all through recorded history, and many students of these movements (some reverent, some irreverent) have attempted to set down the laws that govern them. Some of the greatest revivals of all time took place in Israel in the centuries before Christ. The book of Acts is largely a chronicle of revival. For centuries after the New Testament was written, the church of Jesus Christ subsisted on revival fervor. During the Middle Ages seasons of freshening occurred when God's people ceased trusting in their own righteousness and turned to the Lord. The Reformation of the sixteenth century and the missionary expansion of the eighteenth and nineteenth centuries were the direct products of church revival.

In recent years the subject of spiritual awakening has caught the attention of the psychologist and sociologist, with the unfortunate result that the "excesses" of the revival movement have received more attention than is their due. William James, Edwin Starbuck, J. H. Leuba, and their successors have built up a public distaste for such undignified activities. Even Christians of evangelical persuasion have been raising objections. It has proved difficult to separate the revival spirit from its abuses. Explosions are notoriously hard to contain, and supernatural explosions are no exception. True revivals are instruments of Jesus Power, but they are also very human phenomena. When spiritual awakening comes to a church or community, some are always too easily swayed by it, while others seek to exploit it for personal benefit. Even so, God has used revival in the past, and if we are to believe Scripture he will use it again.

What are some of the laws of revival that have been established in Scripture and tested in experience? One is the prerequisite of *prevailing prayer*. When a remarkable student awakening broke out at Asbury College, Kentucky in February, 1970 it took nearly everyone by surprise. The college president was out of the country. For two weeks the college auditorium was crowded with singing, witnessing, praying students; at four o'clock in the morning the meeting was still going strong. Effects of that revival have been felt all over the world. Not until afterward was it discovered that small, hidden student groups had been meeting early and late, covenanting daily and interceding before God on behalf of their school and its faculty and students.[6] Here, as in all such situations, prayer was not the source of power, but the means. A supernatural source provided the power in answer to prayer.

A second law of revival is that it always deals with *individual souls*. This law coincides with what we saw to be one of Adolf Berle's natural laws of power: namely, that power always accrues to individuals, not to groups.[7] Berle's observation about the personal nature of power is important in view of the continuing attacks by nonevangelicals on "the irrelevance of individualistic piety." A quality of arrogance attaches to such attacks that makes them difficult to refute objectively, but if power is given to individuals, never to groups, it is hard to understand why Christianity should be demeaned because it is individualistic. Dr. W. W. Sweet, the distinguished Methodist church historian, taught that "the basic doctrine in democracy is the emphasis upon individual worth. Likewise one of the basic doctrines of evangelical Christianity is the infinite value which God places upon each individual."[8] Edward M. Hulme has corroborated his view, stating that "society . . . derives its life from individuals who compose it. Individuality, the force of separate selfhood, is the most important fact in human life."[9]

Today the emphasis is away from individual man and toward mass man. Collectivism is being thrust upon society in more and more elaborate forms. Computers now classify numbers instead of names. Young people say they do not wish to become IBM cards; they complain of an "identity crisis." Even the churches have been invaded by an impersonality that has sapped them of spiritual vitality in many cases. Emotionally starved church people, after hearing sermons about "social relevance," spend their evenings weeping not at the altar rails but into their television sets. What is needed to help such people is not less Christian individualism but more!

Jesus Power has tremendous social implications, but its administration by the Holy Spirit is personal, dealing always with individual men and women. Only as individuals are converted will Christianity become relevant to social need. Conversion is not the end, to be sure, but it is certainly the beginning. Without the planting of a seed one can hardly speak of growth.

We saw that the word "mass" when applied to "mass evangelism" is really a misnomer. People are not evangelized in the mass, only as persons.[10] In the same way, when God sends revival he sends it on a One-to-one basis. Finney, Moody, and the other revivalists of the nineteenth century acted on sound principles when they devised ways to deal with individuals among the crowds that came to hear them preach the Gospel. The same principles are followed today by responsible evangelists.

A third law of revival is that *God arranges the timing.* Sometimes a church will put a notice on its bulletin board reading REVIVAL TONIGHT AT 7:30 O'CLOCK. Strictly speaking the announcement is an anachronism, for no church can schedule revival. The same God who controls sidereal time also controls revival time. To be correct the notice should read EVANGELISTIC SERVICE TONIGHT. Admitting that "evangelism" and "revival" sometimes overlap in meaning, one may still draw some valuable distinctions. Evangelism is the preaching of good news, revival is the receiving of new life. Evangelism is what man does for God, revival is what God does for man. Evangelism is sowing, revival is reaping. Evangelism is the carrying out of the Great Commission, revival is the blessing Jesus Christ gives to the work. Evangelism is sharing the gift of God's salvation, revival is cleansing by the power of the Holy Spirit through the blood of Christ. The church is making plans to evangelize the world, but the world is waiting for the church to be revived.

When the Holy Spirit revives a church it goes through a period of self-purification. Sin among the members is confessed and removed. Some make restitution. People give new attention to the study of the Word of God. Jesus Christ assumes preeminence. Manuscripts disappear from the pulpits as pastors preach Christ from the overflow of their hearts. A passion for souls grips church officers whose performance of their duties has become perfunctory. Members awaken to a concern for the neighborhood. Singing is touched with glory as new meaning is poured into the traditional words. Interest quickens in the sacraments and ordinances of the church, and in missionary and social outreach. The budget is oversubscribed. In short, the church wakes up.

For years the fascinating subject of revival has led me on tracking expeditions through religious libraries. My first publishing effort as a Christian, a slim volume which appeared in 1958, was a collection of essays on spiritual awakening. Since then as a member of the Billy Graham team I have witnessed God at work in remarkable ways on nearly every continent: in giant meetings, small Bible study groups, youth rallies, and in other ways. Yet revival—heaven-sent revival—is, as I have tried to suggest, a mysterious and elusive thing that follows no human schedule.

Twice in my lifetime prior to 1971 I encountered what I now know to have been true revival: once during the mid-fifties at Mount Hermon, California during some pastors' meetings led by evangelist Roy Hession of England and the Reverend Armin Gesswein of Pasadena, founder of the Revival Prayer Fellowship; and again in the early 1960's in certain gatherings under the ministry (both in Switzerland and America) of Mr. Festo Kivengere and Mr. William Nagenda of the East Africa Revival. Both times I was touched— wounded in the hollow of the thigh like wrestling Jacob.[11] Yet none of these meetings took place in a local church. As one who was a pastor for many years in low-powered churches I yearned to see a congregation come to life, quickened by the Spirit of God.

Today I can say with the Samaritans of Sychar, "Now we believe, not because of your saying, for we ourselves have heard, and we know."[12] During the late fall of 1971, as I was working on the pages of this chapter, God sent a moving of his Spirit into the churches of our sister cities to the north. Here is the way it came about.

On Wednesday evening, October 13, 1971 in a little Baptist church in Saskatoon, Saskatchewan, twin thirty-seven-year-old evangelists from Mansfield, Ohio—Ralph and Lou Sutera—opened a series of meetings designed to renew the spiritual life of Christians. They preached and sang and invited people to get right with God. They emphasized the facing of one's own sin, the crucifixion of self, the enthronement of Jesus Christ, and the filling of the Holy Spirit. First to respond to the invitation was a lady member of the church whose life was remarkably touched. That was the start of what some are calling the greatest religious awakening in the four-hundred-year history of the church in Canada.

Investigation disclosed that the Suteras' ministry had been unusually blessed in an Evangelical Free Church in Abbotsford, British Columbia two years earlier, and again during September, 1971 in another Evangelical Free Church in Prince George. By late October teams of lay witnesses from these churches began arriving in Saskatoon via jet airliner to tell what God had done in their midst. Then it seemed that things got completely out of hand—out of man's hands, that is. Night after night people crowded to the front of Ebenezer Baptist Church, seeking to get right with God, confessing, weeping, witnessing, singing, sharing, praying, and praising. The audience grew and the meetings moved to larger churches and finally to the civic auditorium. Soon teams of revived Christians were heading for the airport to witness to churches in Regina, Edmonton, Toronto—and Winnipeg.

That's where I came into the picture. I had read accounts of the revival but was not sure what to do about it. In December I received a letter from a friend, Leonard Ravenhill, author and world authority on revival. He had recently returned to his home in Nassau, Bahamas, from Canada. He wrote:

When meetings last until 2 and 3 A.M.; when couples tear up their divorce papers before 1,800 people; when the chief of police reports a rash of crime-confessing; when shopkeepers say they are staggered by the number of folk owning to shoplifting; when lawyers and psychologists get saved; when church members confess they have been living in sin; when all this and more happens night after night for weeks, one might say that there is a touch of revival. Hop a plane, my brother, and get a "foretaste of Glory divine."

I "hopped a plane." On a cold Wednesday evening, December 15, I was present for the services in Winnipeg's Elim Chapel. I arrived at 7:35 o'clock and found the church warm and crowded with over a thousand people. I had to sit in the front row. After some singing and testimonies of people whose lives had been renewed in the past week, the preacher, Wilbert L. McLeod, finally stepped into the pulpit. I studied him carefully. He was fifty-three years old, with a rugged, kindly face. He wore a sweater under his coat jacket. He was a native of Winnipeg, then ministering in Saskatoon, but his church had released him for wider ministry during the revival.

Mr. McLeod spoke in a clear, strong, unaffected voice. He told us that most people think they cannot change, so they settle for something less than what God would have for them; but what man cannot do, God can do. He said that all ways don't lead to God any more than all roads in Canada lead to Winnipeg. There was one door to the ark, and there is one door to God, and that is Christ. He then took us to the third chapter of Colossians and showed us that we can be what God expects us to be—like Christ—but that God asks us to sell out to him on his terms. We don't have anything to give to God; he doesn't need anything from us. We have been sweeping things under the rug, but God has been turning the rug back.

"The power is there," he said. "No man has it; we can only tell you about it. But thank God, we can change. If we mortify the deeds of the body, the Bible promises, we shall live."

Two hours had passed and it seemed like thirty minutes. We sang a hymn, and during the singing people began going forward. No invitation was given. The only words spoken by Mr. McLeod were, "That's right, keep coming." They knelt all around the front of the church, on the platform, by the front seats. I had to move to the second row, then to the third. Over one hundred people came; at least half of them were young.

The meeting adjourned to another church for what was called the "Afterglow." I expected a prayer meeting, and prayer there was, but most of the time the people were "relating to each other." About 120 people were present, sitting in three concentric circles. One empty chair stood in the center. A leader asked if anyone had a spiritual problem. A person would stand up and state a need. The leader would ask, "Can anyone who has been revived in these meetings relate to this problem?" Someone would stand and address the other person across the room with informal counsel, perhaps from the Bible, perhaps from his experience. Then the leader would ask two or three to leave the room and pray with the person who had the need. Others told of marvelous victories after years of spiritual and moral defeat.

Midnight arrived; folks came and went. The crowd moved closer to the center of the circle. People were being helped. Ministers told of problems of pride, and were dealt with like anyone else. No one put on airs. Laymen confessed their hypocrisy and their critical attitudes toward ministers. Great love was present, and acceptance, and forgiveness. People continued to relate to each other. Bursts of song filled the air: "We'll Give the Glory to Jesus,". . ."Jesus Sets Me Absolutely Free."

The meeting went on for another two hours, with individuals coming to the chair in the center, kneeling and sometimes weeping, while others gathered around and laid hands on them in prayer. At 1:30 A.M. I went to my hotel, feeling no fatigue. Within a few days my own life was exposed for what it was; the Spirit convicted and cleansed, and the joy of salvation was restored.

Several phenomena in the Canadian revival deserve attention. In each city the local church was the center of activity. In each church the number of people responding was evenly divided between youth and adults. No efforts were made to "promote" the revival through the communications media. No single preacher or personality dominated the movement; its "missionaries" were laymen as well as clergymen. In the "Afterglow" the emphasis was placed on people helping people. As Ralph Sutera expressed it, "This is group therapy with Christ as the focal point."

Revival as it appears in history has taken different forms, but it generally involves the preaching of judgment and separation from God, confession of sin, repentance, self-crucifixion, the authority of the Scriptures, the atonement of Jesus Christ for sin at the cross, the offer and acceptance of salvation as a free gift, the filling of the Holy Spirit, and the joy and discipline of the Christian life. As the depowering of men and women takes place, people come to their senses and see where their pride has landed them. Christians are praying that in the days immediately ahead multitudes will be in the valley of decision calling upon the name of the Lord. As the cry for help goes up and brokenness before God is evidenced, we believe God will heed and answer. He is not cruel as men are cruel. He will not leave us desolate. He will come with power.

No experience of man on the earth or moon or anywhere else can match the joy of seeing true revival. No wonder we yearn for it! It means that proud, self-assured men and women are brought under conviction by Jesus Power. They bow their heads before an invisible Lord, receive Jesus Christ into their hearts with childlike faith, and enter into his eternal Kingdom. Not only do sinners receive Grace and guilty ones pardon, but hopeless ones are given new heart, confused ones receive clarification, bereaved ones are comforted, the loveless are loved, and the lost are found. When Jesus said, "Receive the Holy Spirit,"[13] he set the classic pattern for revival.

Chapter 14

The Church on Fire

> The disciples of Christ made no impression upon the world until they became a church on fire. After they had prayed earnestly, believed sincerely and waited patiently, divine power was released. The fire from heaven fell upon them. The great spiritual outpouring at Pentecost set the New Testament pattern of revival which has never been altered. . . . The need for the Holy Spirit is no less acute today than it was then. The resources of God are no less abundant now than they were then.[1]
>
> —BILLY GRAHAM

THE church of Jesus Christ today has been given the toughest assignment in the universe: to train and motivate individuals who will confront the human race with its need for God. Setting such a task force in motion requires unbelievable power. All the combustibles in the world, all the latent atomic energy in the Milky Way, could not generate enough power to put one person in the Kingdom of God. Yet a Sunday-school teacher, in the power of the Holy Spirit, can do it in a few minutes.

Men as they are do not want God. They may want some of his fringe benefits, but not the living God himself. They claim that he interferes with their freedom. As they ride their little toboggans toward disaster they keep on playing the power game, trying to gain advantage over each other, ignoring the fact that God in his mercy has thrown them a rope ladder of salvation. That's the way men are and that's the way they will stay, until and unless each is born anew individually and in his own way of the Spirit of God.

Lightning struck the steeple of a church, and the village atheist went out to watch it burn. He was reproached by the minister with the words, "You never came to our church before"—to which the man retorted, "Your church was never on fire before." If the church is to carry out its task it must be struck by lightning and set afire. Nothing less will prove adequate. The flames of Pentecost are the norm. The burning church will not merely attract the atheist; it will also show him his pride and error and lead him to the truth. The church on fire can do anything, but when the fire is doused by the things of this world, the church can hardly pay its bills. The spiritual flame that kindles the church does not flicker and die out because of lack of fuel, but rather because it is smothered. Such fire, given a chance, is like the burning bush that Moses saw in the desert— *arderet et non combureretur* ("it burns without being consumed"). Why not? God's resources are infinite. A group of churches in East Africa has been in revival for twenty years, and no signs of abatement have yet appeared.

The church (if I may update George Fox) does not consist of steel, glass, concrete, foam rubber, air conditioning, and blacktop.[2] The church is people with a message. Now, what does that message offer man that he does not already have? What can the church that is spiritually aglow contribute to the sociocultural scene? Many things, but in the interest of good communication I shall consider three:

1. *Victory through power.* Victory is usually thought of today in terms of sport. Professional football teams are so popular in America that metropolitan police are reporting drops in crime statistics on Monday evenings during the playing season. The reason is that an important league game is being televised nationally. Football as a spectator sport appeals to millions because it is the perfect medium for acting out the human power game. The quarterback is Everyman; the opposing defense is the competitor across the aisle or across the street. Recently one of the more successful coaches of the National Football League remarked that the game was "10 percent

physical and 90 percent mental," by which he meant that desire wins more games than either skill or fitness. The prospect of victory is a prime source of power.

Victory is precisely what Jesus Christ provides. The Christian with Jesus Power cannot lose. He may look like a loser, he may appear to act like a loser, the world may reckon him a loser, but in God's book he is a winner undefeated and untied. The reason is that he is playing a different game, in a different ball park, under a different coach. The opponent is not his fellow man but the accuser of all men. Running interference for the Christian is the Spirit of God. As he takes the hand-off from life, the Christian finds in his mouth the sweet, sweet taste of victory. Jesus said, "In the world ye shall have tribulation: but be of good cheer; I have overcome the world."[3]

Has a man just lost his job? Has a youth suffered a permanent disability? Has a wife learned that her husband is unfaithful? Are children a disappointment? Jesus Christ offers to such more than consolation: he gives the power to triumph over circumstances. As Isaiah said, God gives "power to the faint":[4] to the depressed, the sick, the aging, the lonely, the bereaved, the orphaned, the imprisoned, the disfranchised, the underprivileged, the victims of war and fire and flood and man's inhumanity. Jesus not only knows the trouble we feel, he gives us strength to pull out of it. Millions of people have found such victory over the vicissitudes of daily living through Jesus Christ.

But others remain unconvinced. When they hear a testimony to Jesus Power, they have a reply that goes like this: "You're lucky, you have religion. You think everything will work out, or at least you pretend you do. Of course life is not like that. You can float into a dream world and close your eyes to grim reality, but that doesn't change the facts. I guess if you can swallow all that stuff it's OK, but I can't see it."

It's not a question of changing facts or pretending what isn't so, it's a matter of gaining access to power. The Christian life is not built on the premise that "things will work out," it is built on a cross. The

Gospel promises not a happy issue of circumstances but victory over circumstances. Amy Carmichael stepped into a freshly dug pit one evening as she was approaching her cottage on a mission station in India. She spent the next twenty-one years in bed—in pain.[5] Yet out of that agonizing experience came inspiring verses of encouragement that have helped people all over the world. For Amy Carmichael the prospect of victory in Christ was a prime source of power.

2. *Joy through power.* Martin Luther once remarked that most people have just enough religion to keep them from getting pleasure out of their sin, but not enough to give them any real joy in believing. Joy is the most underworked word in the Christian message; yet the New Testament uses it lavishly. The magi had joy when they saw the star over Jerusalem.[6] Joy sent Jesus Christ to the cross.[7] The disciples had joy when they saw the risen Lord. There was joy in Samaria after Philip preached forgiveness through the cross of Christ.[8] Paul defined the Kingdom of God as joy[9] and the fruit of the Spirit as joy.[10] The New Testament itself was composed in a spirit of joy.[11] Says A. W. Tozer, "The book of Acts is almost hilarious with joy."[12]

Now notice something rather peculiar about these references to joy: Each is connected directly to spiritual power. In no case is the joy synthetic or whipped-up; our brothers and sisters in the early church did not attempt to create a mood by "getting happy." The joy was a result of supernatural intervention that effected a change in human lives. God was at work in history in a remarkable way.

"The chief end of man," says the Westminster Shorter Catechism in its finest moment, "is to glorify God and enjoy him forever." Set a church on fire and it produces joy—not because it is a great church or a friendly church, or because it provides a diversified ministry for differing age groups, but because of what God is doing in its midst. The congregation places itself on the altar of God and is no longer expending its energy trying to please men. Instead it is bending itself to tap a higher source of power. "Bend the church!" was the watchword of the Welsh Revival of 1904–1906, and God honored that work. He built a fire in Wales that warmed churches not only in

Britain and Europe, but in India, California, Siberia, and other parts of the world.

The fire of God cleanses and purifies his people and burns away that in the church which is unworthy. But that is not all it does. Fire also provides a warm climate conducive to making new Christians. I have never heard of a soul being born into a cold church. Spiritual fire in the pulpit sends a shower of sparks into the pew. Here and there a blaze is kindled; someone confesses Christ as Savior, and the congregation responds. Some members turn radiant. They sense that their church is doing at last what it was born to do. A fresh testimony revives the faith of the believers in other congregations who learn what is happening.

Joy, then, is a response to spiritual power at work. It does not depend upon innovations in the church program. It does not require a gifted song leader. Dancing in the aisles is no sure sign of God's presence. Charged emotions can generate excitement, but true enthusiasm comes only from being *entheos,* that is to say, *in God.* When the Creator of the universe is at work he sends joy through power.

3. *Rest through power.* The paradox of faith is that the church on fire is the church at rest. When a congregation finds itself in the will of God, a marvelous peace comes over the people. The usual human effort and struggle die away. No longer do men's standards supersede God's standards. Activity goes on; the sacraments and ordinances are observed; boards and committees continue to meet, but there is a holy hush over it all even in the midst of promotion and preparation for great events. God is taken actively into account. He assumes the leadership. His directive will is sought, and the people learn to follow his commands.

Is there a disciplinary problem? The church turns to Galatians 6:1: "Brethren, if a man be overtaken in fault, ye which are spiritual, restore such an one in the spirit of meekness; considering thyself, lest thou also be tempted."[13] Is there a financial problem? The church turns to 2 Corinthians 8 and 9. Is there a problem of division? The church turns to 1 John 3:11: "This is the message which you have heard from the beginning, that we should love one another."[14] Does the human element break down? For example, does a visiting speaker fail to appear? There is no disappointment, for the congregation is waiting not upon man but upon God. It accepts his provision. The meeting goes on. God is present and his people are at rest.

The subject of rest takes up much of the Letter to the Hebrews. We find that to Moses and the Israelites, during their long sojourn in the desert, Canaan was not only the land of promise, it was the place of rest. "Canaan rest" was to be a rest from forty years of wandering. Rest meant not just inertia; it meant safe borders so that they could till the land, bring up their children, and worship God.

We learn however that very few of the Israelites who were delivered from Egypt made it into the land of Canaan. Disobedience and rebelliousness toward God kept most of them from entering. The word used by the author of Hebrews to explain their predicament is derived from *dunamis.* They were not *able* to enter the land of rest because they lacked the power. Who was to supply the power? God, but they had turned away from him. Without God's help they could not cross the Jordan, they could not establish the borders; and without safe borders rest was impossible.

Today the analogy holds. Rest for the Christian means inner peace —peace of mind, peace of soul, peace with God and man. No matter what strife goes on in the world, the Christian can set about his tasks in serenity of spirit. He knows that God is securing his borders, maintaining his inner sanctuary, and enabling him at any time to get into immediate contact with the unseen source of supply. Rest is made possible through God's mighty power.

Recently a group of clergymen attended a denominational refresher course in Kansas City. They listened to a series of radical speakers, one of whom, after ridiculing what he considered the ineptness of local congregations in dealing with social issues, told the ministers, "If I were you I would go home and burn down my church." The Apostle Paul had a better idea. He wrote to Timothy, "Build a fire under the gift of God that is within you."[15]

It is not the building that needs the torch, but the members. It is not the institution that needs power, but the individuals who make it up. Fire out of control spreads destruction and calamity, but fire under control brings warmth and growth. No matter how many killing frosts have numbed a congregation, the fire of love can cause a thaw, breaking down old animosities, reestablishing human relationships, creating fellowship in the Spirit. (In Regina, when it was proposed that separate revival meetings be held for youth, the young people objected. Love had snapped shut the generation gap.) The fire of love burns away the artificial distinctions that men set up, so that people can treat each other as brothers and sisters in Christ. (In Winnipeg laymen preached from the pulpit while ministers took up the offering.) The fire of love sends up in smoke the centuries-old history of prejudice and establishes a genuine equality among people of different sexes and races. (In Richmond, Virginia a distinguished southern white lady walked forward during a crusade to commit her life to Christ. She was counseled by a trained volunteer who happened to be a black lady. Afterward the new inquirer was asked by a friend, "Wasn't that a colored person who was counseling you?" She replied in the freshness of her faith, "To be honest, I never noticed.") The fire of love pierces the conscience, forcing a man to examine himself and to make things right. (In Capetown, South Africa the sheriff had to rent an extra warehouse after a 1966 Bantu revival to take care of returned stolen goods. In Saskatoon, Canada, during the 1971 revival, a large department store, Simpsons-Sears Ltd., had to open a special account to post the returns from shoplifters making restitution.)

It is not the building that needs the torch, but the members. It is not the institution that needs power, but the individuals who make it up. What kind of power? Power for victory, for joy, for rest. Love power. Jesus Power.[16]

Chapter 15

Power Ready and Available

> Dear brothers and sisters, let us be strong through the
> mighty power of the Lord. Let us profess our faith with
> courage and spread the Gospel with zeal. Let us be pre-
> pared to be faithful to the Lord at any cost. Don't be
> cowards! Don't be weary! Don't give way! Don't com-
> promise! The battle is indeed furious, but God's glory
> will be manifest there. Hark! The trumpet has been
> blown. Look! The victory is in sight.[1]
>
> —WANG MING-TAO

WE have nearly finished our brief tour of the Grand Tetons of
power. Unfortunately you have had to put up with an amateur guide.
Many questions have been raised, and I am aware of an incapacity
to answer them. While I have tried not to stray beyond my own field
of competence (whatever that is), even that has proved impossible.
But wait a moment—

D. T. Niles once defined evangelism as one beggar telling another
beggar where to find food. Niles was a Ceylonese from the mystic
East; I am a conventional pragmatist living in the American Midwest,
but I identify with his approach. The question is not, What is Jesus
Power? but rather, How do you turn on the faucet? Not, Why is the
church in its present condition? but rather, How do you hook on to
the supply chute? Beneath the prairie of our church life runs a
subterranean stream of living water with plenty for all. Once we sink
a shaft, the parched desert will blossom as the rose. How do we do
it? How do we become involved in miracle? For Christ promised

that even today his power will perform mighty acts, and each new day brings its own evidence. As one Christian said of his Master, "He may not have changed my water into wine, but he has changed my beer into furniture."

People want to know whether the power that the Bible describes is released at conversion or later; whether it is a temporary or a permanent supply; whether some kind of spiritual litmus paper is available by which one may determine whether it is the "real thing." When we turn to the Word of God we find guidelines to wisdom in this area, but no simplistic answers. Certainly Jesus is always ready to release his power into men, and thousands of Christians can testify that a supernatural enabling and strengthening was given them at conversion. But thousands of other Christians cannot even tell at what precise moment they were converted. The direction of their lives was changed—no question about that—and they are also aware that God is now using them in a powerful way. But did the power come at conversion? They are not sure. Was there some kind of "second blessing"? They are not sure of that either. But I would add a third question: Does it matter? As long as the conduit is functioning, we need only to praise God and carry on. As for the litmus paper test, George Whitefield asked some questions of his eighteenth-century hearers that will serve equally well today.

Has God wrought in you not only a deep sense of the outward acts of sin, but a humbling sense of the inward corruptions of your heart? Has he led you beyond the streams, by the powerful operations of his Spirit, to the fountainhead? Has God wrought in you a spirit of zeal and love? Has he wrought in you a love for his name, a zeal for his cause? Has he wrought in your heart a deadness to the world so that you can live above it from morning till night? Has he wrought in you a love for his people—not people of your persuasion only; has he wrought in you a love for your enemies? What do you say?[2]

Some will object to applying the term "Jesus Power" to the men and women of God in the Old Testament. They are right; the distinction is worth making. The Bible tells us that all through Hebrew history people were conscious of the Holy Spirit's presence and power, yet after Pentecost the disciples knew him in a different way. But the Spirit himself did not change. It really matters little how one labels power from God. The irrigation ditch is not too concerned how the liquid flowing through it is to be called; the important thing is that something life-giving is going between the banks.

Hosea wrote regarding Jacob the patriarch, "He had power with God."[3] Micah the prophet said, "I am full of power by the Spirit of the Lord . . . to declare unto . . . Israel his sin."[4] David sang with his lyre, "The God of Israel is he that giveth strength and power unto his people."[5] Isaiah's soliloquy on power ranks with the finest utterances in recorded literature:

He giveth power to the faint; and to them that have no might he increaseth strength. Even the youths shall faint and be weary, and the young men shall utterly fall. But they that wait upon the Lord shall renew their strength; they shall mount up with wings as eagles; they shall run, and not be weary; and they shall walk, and not faint.[6]

By a kind of inner history these descriptions belong to the same family as Paul's declaration to the Philippian Christians:

I count all things but loss for the excellency of the knowledge of Christ Jesus my Lord . . . that I may know him, and the power of his resurrection, and the fellowship of his sufferings.[7]

Nowhere outside the Bible is such power recognized. Archaeologists, historians, linguists, sociologists, and literary critics may scrutinize the sacred books from beginning to end; they may divide them and subdivide them, compare them with cognate languages, and subject them to every scientific approach imaginable, without coming within a country mile of the power Biblical writers were talking about. A noted German professor of church history remarked, when his nation's adventure in higher criticism was at its zenith, that there were ten thousand servant girls in Berlin who knew more about

Jesus Christ than any theologian living.[8] Our Lord himself said much the same thing.[9]

John warns us that we are to "believe not every spirit" but rather we are to "try the spirits whether they are of God."[10] John's inspired advice is to be followed, and yet we cannot spend all our time running tests, as they sometimes seem to do in hospitals. The power must be put to use or we shall end up like those befuddled souls whom Paul pictures as "ever learning and never able to come to the knowledge of the truth."[11] The best way to test a spirit, like a new car, is to turn the key in the ignition. Jesus said a tree would be known by its fruit, and that if a man got to work and did God's will, he would soon "know the doctrine."

One Sunday morning in August a few years ago I was asked to fill the pulpit of a suburban congregation in the Midwest. Although it was not the custom in that church, I told the people that if they meant business for Jesus Christ I wanted to see them down front. Then I announced the invitation hymn and the organist struck up an unfamiliar tune. It disconcerted me, for I felt the hymn was quite unsingable, and I tried to catch the organist's eye. At last she looked my way, raised her eyebrows, smiled, and nodded. I looked again at the hymnbook and realized that she was only following directions —I had made an error in announcing the hymn number. By the time I finally looked to the front of the pulpit, I found to my complete astonishment that over thirty people had gathered quietly and were standing with bowed heads. Some other power had been at work.

Thousands of people walking the streets of our cities and towns would like to do business with Jesus Christ. They yearn for a vital inner strength that will give their lives meaning beyond daily events. They have a loose connection with a church, but they feel God has something better in view for them than their present spiritual condition. They know, too, what is holding them back. Perhaps it is a habit they would like to shake but can't seem to. Perhaps it is a doubt that has been festering in their mind ever since reading a book critical of Christ, the Bible, and the Gospel. Perhaps it is a personal animus toward a particular clergyman. Whatever the reason, it is rooted in self-love and pride, and they have let it neutralize them spiritually as a policeman's use of mace neutralizes a street rioter.

I have learned that Jesus Christ has made available to everyone who trusts in him a supernatural empowerment beyond the imagination of man. I repeat, I have no special understanding in this area. Holy men have spent their lifetimes in such research; theologians, linguists, copyists, schoolmen, have examined the truth of Christianity with infinite pains and care for nearly two thousand years. I am a journalist who has spent a few hours in the library. I have never been to the third heaven, or even to the first, and have probably given out the wrong tune more than once. *But what does it matter if Jesus Power comes through?*

The charge has been made—and it is probably true—that when preachers talk about the Holy Spirit they say either too little or too much. Who, after all, is sufficient for these things?[12] Who can know the hidden counsels of God? Who can track down the original sources of divine activity? The prologue to the book of Job offers a tantalizing glimpse—but that is all—of the supernatural background to our human life on earth. We find God and Satan discussing the character of Job and his ability to stand up under adversity. We note that after Satan has taunted the Lord for "hedging" Job with protection, the Lord says to Satan, "Behold, all that he has is in your power."[13] But Job does not turn against God; in the midst of his trials and questionings he says, "Though he slay me, yet will I trust him."[14]

Every time we try to penetrate the mystery of God's power—through drugs for example—we are beaten back in despair. We simply do not have enough information to form conclusions about the manner and method of God's dispensation of power. Furthermore, it is not our business to know the *how* and *why* and *where* and *what,* for God knows the tendency of man in his pride to take over upon any pretext. The Apostle Paul said that God will deliver the creature who tries to usurp the role of Creator to "vile affections"

and "a reprobate mind."[15] Our concern should be with the *here* and
now, for God has also told us (if I may paraphrase) that if we simply
trust him and man the intake valves, he will not leave us desolate.
He will send power, for he is the God of follow-through. Then when
the power does come it turns out that we don't have it at all, but
rather that the power has us!

Our study began with a consideration of the human power game.
We discovered that some of the principles Adolf Berle has applied
to human power also relate to the extrahuman forces that have
occupied our attention. Let us look now at some of Berle's conclud-
ing comments:

> Power is essential to order. . . .
> Power is not the producer, is not the merchant, is not the teacher, is not
> the painter, is not the musician. . . . Power is a tool only. . . .
> Power is less important for what it does than for the forces it releases.
> The real function of power and the order it creates is the liberation of men
> and women to think and be and make the most of themselves. . . .
> Power [comes to men and women] in the measure to which they give
> resources for greater development to those with whom they have contact.[16]

These reflections, composed in retirement by a former U.S. Assis-
tant Secretary of State and lifelong government official, do not say
much about the sources of power, but they tell us a great deal about
its operation. For example, if we apply the expression, "Power is
essential to order," to the ecumenical movement it will help explain
why so many attempts at church union are in difficulty today. If we
reflect upon Berle's remark about the function of power to liberate,
it may clear up the confusion that surrounds the currently popular
theological doctrine of "reconciliation." The New Testament speaks
of man being reconciled to God through Christ, particularly in 2
Corinthians 5, but as John A. Mackay has pointed out, *reconciliation*
is not the only important word in the Christian lexicon. Equally
significant is *redemption,* a commerical word used in the first century
to describe the transaction of buying a slave's freedom.[17] Applied to

the work of Christ on the cross, redemption signifies an act of liberation. Power liberates; Jesus Power liberates us from our sins at Calvary. That is the heart of the Gospel. Any number of terms such as reconciliation, peace, and union with Christ can be helpful in illustrating our new relationship with God and with our fellow man, but when we are dealing with the issues of sin and death, we must look for words that carry power.

Other spiritual truths can be derived from Berle's secular conclusions. When he speaks of power as being "a tool only," we are reminded that Jesus Power is not some kind of gnostic emanation to be idolized or exploited. It is simply energy made available for use. If we worship it we are done for. When he tells us that power is not as important as the forces it releases, it suggests to us that Jesus Power is an inexhaustible supply of social and political motivation for the alleviation of human misery and the building of peaceful bridges between men and nations.

Finally Berle tells us that power is awarded to those who provide others with "resources for greater development." Translated into the thought-forms of Scripture, his words describe the abundant life which is the fruit of love in action. Love "seeketh not her own," as Paul says.[18] Love is interested in the welfare of other men. It would be correct to define evangelism as the Christian means of offering people resources for greater development through the infusion of power from on high. Thus evangelism is really an expression of both divine and human love; and Jesus Power is another way of speaking of love power. If we are wondering whether the power at work in a particular situation is of God or not, we need simply to look for the love. Lady Julian of Norwich expressed it long ago in her quiet and classic way:

Everything has its being by the love of God; that is, God made all things for love, and by the same love he keeps them. And until a man is willing to make himself nothing, for love, to obtain him who is everything, he is unable to obtain spiritual rest.[19]

Our exciting brush with power is over, but I hear one plaintive, insistent voice that carries above everything that has been said: "What about me? I don't feel any particular goosebumps. I believe in Jesus. I pray. Sundays you will find me in church. When Billy Graham came to our town I sang in his choir every night. I try to witness to my faith, but my life has been one disappointment after another, and most of the time I feel absolutely powerless."

If the principles set forth in these pages are sound, they should help such a person. Powerless is exactly the way God wants us to feel! I once heard a speaker attempt to describe the Christian life in these terms: "We try, and try, and try, and keep on trying, and fall down, and pick ourselves up, and try again." What a dismal drift! When human power is used to fill a superhuman role it is David fighting in Saul's armor. Naturally it ends in frustration. Contrast that description with what I heard in a small meeting during the Winnipeg revival. A man confessed that he was having trouble maintaining a Christian attitude toward his minister. The man leading the meeting said, "Sorry, we can't help you. But we know who can."

The person who feels "absolutely powerless" may actually be misrepresenting his condition; instead of being powerless, he may be generating too much of the wrong kind of power. But in most cases the feeling of powerlessness is due to another cause. Rather than become preachy at this point, let me relate a baseball story I read years ago. As I recall, it was titled "The Fifty Thousand Dollar Fly." (I thought it was one of Ring Lardner's, but have been unable to trace it.) It seems a young rube from the country was signed by a major league club because he was a sensation at the plate. His fielding was weak, so he was assigned to right field where he barely managed to hold down the position. In due course his team won the pennant and entered the World Series. When the games were even at three apiece, the country boy's team led going into the ninth inning of the deciding game. He took his place in right field for the last inning and the opponents began filling the bases. Then with two out, the batter lifted an easy fly ball to right field. Our man from the country reached for it with his gloved hand, bobbled it, and finally dropped it. The World Series was over. The team had lost. Instead of heading for the dugout the other players clustered around the right fielder for an explanation. The manager joined them. He said, "Open up your hand," and the young man obliged. The ungloved hand held a half-dozen peanuts.

Usually what is keeping us from Jesus Power is peanuts. We allow what is small and insignificant to get in the way—some sin that seems so petty as to be ridiculous, but which the devil can use—and the power is blocked. Peanuts will never satisfy a hearty appetite. Jesus told us to cultivate that kind of appetite—a spiritual appetite—by hungering and thirsting after righteousness. In the same way the Lord God said to the prophet Jeremiah, "You will seek me, and find me; when you seek me with all your heart."[20] The Psalmist responded to God's challenge by declaring, "When thou saidst, Seek ye my face; my heart said unto thee, Thy face, Lord, will I seek."[21]

The Holy Spirit does not invade a personality as a dictator's secret police break into a man's house. If someone seems to be banging on the door, that could be the beating of your own expectant heart, for the Holy Spirit comes only to those who yearn for him. In a sense the Lord never helps those who help themselves, for he never sends power where it is not desperately wanted. Even when our spiritual craving is at its most acute, he subjects us first to that depowering which will make us poor in spirit. As Lady Julian says, he makes us "nothing for love." He resists the proud that he may give grace to the humble.[22] He crucifies the spirit of self in us that he may fill us with the Spirit of God.

Well, what about it? Power is ready and available and suited exactly to our requirements. The hour is late. The time is ripe. What are we waiting for?

Notes

Preface

1. See pp. 88–97.
2. Sherwood E. Wirt, *The Social Conscience of the Evangelical* (New York: Harper & Row, 1968).
3. Robert McAfee Brown of Stanford University, who made the statement, explains: "This is the reflection of a point of view I generally share. Taken by itself, it is subject of course to serious midunderstandings. . . ." (in a letter to the author, January 18, 1972).
4. Hendrik Kraemer, in a speech at the Assembly Hall, Edinburgh, Scotland, February 1951.
5. Jeremiah 32:17 (KJV).
6. Cf. 2 Corinthians 6:2.

Chapter 1. The Power Game

1. Sherwood E. Wirt, *Love Song: Augustine's Confessions for Modern Man* (New York: Harper & Row, 1971), Book 9, Section 4, p. 120.
2. Friedrich Nietzsche, *Thus Spake Zarathustra.*
3. Cf. Benjamin Disraeli, *Endymion,* Chapter 82.
4. Cf. Edmund Burke, *Letter to a Member of the National Assembly.*
5. John Locke, *Two Treatises of Government,* I.
6. Ecclesiastes 2:4–9, 11 (KJV).
7. Augustine, *City of God,* Book 12, Chapter 6; Book 14, Chapter 13.
8. Cf. 1 Peter 5:5 (KJV).
9. Genesis 3:5 (RSV).
10. Cf. Romans 1:25.
11. Reinhold Niebuhr, *The Nature and Destiny of Man,* 1 (New York: Charles Scribner's Sons; Welwyn, England: James Nisbet & Co. Ltd., 1941), pp. 201, 190–91.
12. Stephen Potter, *Some Notes on Lifemanship* (London: Rupert Hart-Davis, 1950), pp. 14–15.

114

13. Eric Berne, *Games People Play* (New York: Grove Press, 1964), p. 126.
14. 1 John 2:16 (KJV).

Chapter 2. What Men Want

1. Charles C. Ryrie, *The Holy Spirit* (Chicago: Moody Press, 1965), p. 7.
2. Lord Acton (John Emerich Dalberg); in letter to Bishop Mandell Creighton, 1887.
3. Romans 1:21–24, 28 (TEV).
4. I came across this quotation in 1950 in the British Museum, but was not able later to trace its source.
5. Charles A. Reich, *The Greening of America* (New York: Random House, 1970; Bantam Books, 1971), p. 418.
6. John Chrysostom, *Homilies on the Gospel of St. John,* XXVIII, 2.
7. William James, *Varieties of Religious Experience.*
8. See *Decision* magazine, September 1971, p. 3.
9. Jerome, Letter 22, Section 7.

Chapter 3. The Bang or the Whimper

1. Quoted in Lionel B. Fletcher, *The Effective Evangelist* (New York: George H. Doran Co., 1923), p. 93.
2. Vernon C. Grounds, *Revolution and the Christian Faith* (New York: J. B. Lippincott Co., 1971), pp. 130–31.
3. Quoted in William Ernest Hocking, *Strength of Men and Nations* (New York: Harper & Brothers, 1959), p. 74.
4. *Ibid.,* p. 73.
5. Romans 13:1 (Phillips).
6. See Wirt, *Social Conscience of the Evangelical,* pp. 65–78.
7. Christopher Marlowe, *Tamburlaine the Great,* Part II, Act IV, Scene 1.
8. Acts 5:29 (KJV).
9. Thomas Wolfe, *Look Homeward, Angel* (New York: Charles Scribner's Sons; London: Wm. Heinemann, Ltd., 1957), pp. 493–94.
10. Ladislas Farago, *Patton: Ordeal and Triumph* (New York: Ivan Obolensky, 1963), pp. 318 ff.
11. Carl Gustav Jung, *Modern Man in Search of a Soul,* W. S. Dell and Cary F. Baynes, trans. (London: Kegan Paul, Trench, Trubner & Co., 1947), p. 236.

12.   T. S. Eliot, "The Hollow Men," V, *The Complete Poems and Plays, 1909–1950* (New York: Harcourt Brace Jovanovich, Inc.; London: Faber & Faber, Ltd., 1962), p. 59.

Chapter 4. Jesus Power Defined

1.   James R. McIntire, *The Life of the Holy Spirit* (St. Louis, Mo.: Bethany Press, 1930), p. 143.
2.   Cf. Mark 10:42-43.
3.   John 16:7 (RSV).
4.   Cf. Zechariah 4:6.
5.   Matthew 7:29 (KJV).
6.   Mark 2:10 (RSV).
7.   Luke 9:1.
8.   Cf. John 1:12.
9.   Cf. John 17:1-2.
10.   Colossians 1:18.
11.   Ephesians 1:21 (RSV).
12.   Philippians 2:10.
13.   Hebrews 2:14.
14.   Cf. 1 Peter 4:11.
15.   Cf. Matthew 26:53.
16.   Blaise Pascal, *Provincial Letters,* No. 5.
17.   John 14:15 (RSV).
18.   John 5:46 (Phillips).
19.   Bertrand Russell, *Power: A New Social Analysis* (New York: W. W. Norton & Co., 1938), p. 35.

Chapter 5. God's Dynamite

1.   "Be Thou My Vision," Mary Byrne, trans., *Scottish Psalter and Church Hymnary* (London: Oxford University Press, 1929), No. 477, p. 570.
2.   Cf. Mark 12:24.
3.   See also Chapter 12.
4.   Jeremiah 23:29 (RSV).
5.   Hebrews 4:12 (KJV).
6.   Adolf A. Berle, *Power* (New York: Harcourt Brace Jovanovich, Inc., 1967), p. 37.

7. Luke 1:35.

8. Luke 8:43-48.

9. Matthew 6:13 (KJV).

10. 1 Corinthians 4:20 (KJV).

11. Romans 1:4 (KJV).

12. Ephesians 3:7 (KJV).

13. 2 Timothy 1:7 (KJV).

14. Matthew 11:20.

15. Mark 14:62 (RSV).

16. Romans 1:16.

17. 1 Corinthians 1:24 (KJV).

18. Cf. 1 Corinthians 2:4-5.

19. Cf. 1 Thessalonians 1:5.

20. Philippians 3:10.

21. Cf. 2 Timothy 1:8.

22. "There is much suffering in Acts. . . . The power in Acts may be called power in prison" (Frederick Dale Bruner, *A Theology of the Holy Spirit* [Grand Rapids, Mich.: William B. Eerdmans Publishing Co., 1970], p. 190).

23. Acts 3:6 (KJV).

24. Cf. Acts 3:12.

25. Acts 4:7 (RSV).

26. Cf. Acts 4:10.

27. Cf. Acts 8:18-21.

28. Cf. 1 Peter 1:5.

29. Hebrews 7:16 (RSV).

30. Revelation 5:12-13 (KJV).

Chapter 6. The Depowering of Man

1. Thomas Hooker, *The Soules Implantation into the Naturall Olive,* published in London in 1640, Essay 57.15, p. 24.

2. *Decision* magazine, May 1972, p. 2.

3. Berle, *Power,* p. 29.

4. Matthew 5:3 (KJV).

5. Some of the thoughts expressed in this paragraph have been drawn

from my earlier volume *Magnificent Promise* (Chicago: Moody Press, 1964).

6. Roy and Revel Hession, *The Calvary Road* (Philadelphia and London: Christian Literature Crusade, 1950), pp. 29–30.

7. Cf. 2 Corinthians 12:9.

8. Quoted in J. Oswald Sanders, *Spiritual Problems* (Chicago: Moody Press, 1971), p. 60.

9. Cf. Matthew 16:24.

10. Cf. Luke 24:49.

11. Cf. Acts 1:8.

12. Harold J. Ockenga, *Power Through Pentecost,* in *Preaching for Today* (Grand Rapids, Mich.: William B. Eerdmans Publishing Co., 1959), p. 23.

Chapter 7. Plan A and Plan B

1. *Letters of the Rev. Samuel Rutherford,* A. A. Bonar, ed. (New York: Robert Carter & Brothers, 1861), pp. 215, 364, 451.

2. Niccolò Machiavelli, *The Prince,* W. K. Marriott, trans., Chapter 3.

3. Leon Morris, *Spirit of the Living God* (London: Inter-Varsity Press, 1960), p. 51.

4. Samuel Chadwick, *The Way to Pentecost* (London: Hodder & Stoughton, 1932), p. 59.

5. Quoted in Sanders, *Spiritual Problems,* p. 49.

6. Cf. Mark 10:42-43.

7. Cf. Mark 10:43-44.

8. Cf. Luke 13:3.

9. Ralph W. Harris, *The Holy Spirit,* students' manual (Springfield, Mo.: Gospel Publishing House, 1963), p. 24.

10. 2 Corinthians 4:7 (KJV).

11. *Decision* magazine, May 1972, p. 2.

12. Ecclesiastes 9:11 (KJV).

13. Job 38:4 (KJV).

14. Job 40:4; 42:2-3, 6 (KJV).

15. John 2:5 (RSV).

16. G. Campbell Morgan, *The Spirit of God* (New York: Fleming H. Revell Co., 1900), p. 231.

Chapter 8. The Spirit of Power

1. Quoted in C. E. Vulliamy, *John Wesley* (London: Geoffrey Bles, 1931), p. 95.
2. Quoted in J. Oswald Sanders, *The Holy Spirit and His Gifts* (Grand Rapids, Mich.: Zondervan Publishing Co., 1970), p. 10.
3. Chadwick, *Way to Pentecost*, p. 14.
4. Billy Graham, *Peace with God* (Garden City, N.Y.: Doubleday & Co., 1953), p. 89.
5. Morris, *Spirit of the Living God*, pp. 35–36.
6. John 3:8 (KJV).
7. Bernard Ramm, *The Witness of the Spirit* (Grand Rapids, Mich.: William B. Eerdmans Publishing Co., 1959), p. 91.
8. 1 John 2:1 (KJV).
9. Morgan, *Spirit of God*, pp. 203–206.
10. Romans 8:26-27 *(The Living Bible)*.
11. Norman P. Grubb, *Rees Howells, Intercessor* (Fort Washington, Pa.: Christian Literature Crusade, 1952).
12. W. A. Criswell, *The Holy Spirit in Today's World* (Grand Rapids, Mich.: Zondervan Publishing Co., 1966), pp. 82–83.
13. Berle, *Power*, p. 37.
14. Mark 16:20 (KJV).
15. Cf. 1 Corinthians 2:4.
16. C. S. Lewis, *Miracles* (New York: The Macmillan Co., 1947), pp. 125–28.
17. Cf. 1 Corinthians 12—14.
18. Ephesians 3:20 (KJV).

Chapter 9. The Great Power Failure

1. Reuben A. Torrey, *The Power of Prayer* (Grand Rapids, Mich.: Zondervan Publishing Co., 1971), p. 21.
2. Luke 9:43 (KJV).
3. Cf. Matthew 17:19.
4. Karl Barth, *The Epistle to the Romans*, Edwyn C. Hoskyns, trans. (London: Oxford University Press, 1933), pp. 65–66, 72.
5. 2 Timothy 3:5 (KJV).

6. Cf. Revelation 2:4-5.
7. *George Fox's Journal,* Percy Livingstone Parker, ed. (London: Isbister & Co., 1903), pp. 21–22.
8. Lesslie Newbigin, *The Household of God* (New York: Friendship Press, 1954), p. 95.
9. Samuel M. Shoemaker, *With the Holy Spirit and with Fire* (New York: Harper & Row, 1960), pp. 12–13.
10. See Chapter 7.
11. 2 Timothy 3:5 (KJV).
12. Confirmed in a letter to the author, dated January 31, 1972.

Chapter 10. The Jesus People

1. Duane C. Pederson, *The Jesus People* (Glendale, Calif.: Regal Books, 1971), p. 45.
2. Romans 11:33 (KJV).
3. In an interview in Oakland, California, July 1971.
4. Colossians 2:14-15.
5. Psalm 76:10.
6. Edward E. Plowman, *The Jesus Movement in America* (Elgin, Ill.: David C. Cook Publishing Co.; London: Hodder & Stoughton Ltd., 1971), p. 124.
7. Cf. Acts 2:13-15.
8. *The National Baptist Pulpit,* Maynard P. Turner, Jr., ed. (Nashville: Townsend Press, 1969–70), p. 66.
9. Quoted in Norman P. Grubb, *C. T. Studd: Athlete and Pioneer* (Grand Rapids, Mich.: Zondervan Publishing Co., 1939), p. 172.

Chapter 11. The Word of Power

1. This man, an Assemblies of God layman, worked with me on a wartime construction project in California in the summer of 1942.
2. Lloyd C. Douglas, *Magnificent Obsession* (Boston: Houghton Mifflin Co., 1966), pp. 131–35.
3. Psalm 33:6.
4. Exodus 24:3.
5. John 1:1 ff.
6. *Nave's Topical Bible* (Chicago: Moody Press, 1921), p. 1416.

7. Hebrews 1:3 (KJV).
8. J. B. Phillips, *Letters to Young Churches* (New York: The Macmillan Co., 1947), p. xii.
9. Romans 10:17 (KJV).
10. This extemporaneous statement was made during a question period at the Inter-Varsity Student Missionary Convention at Urbana, Ill., in December 1964. It appeared in *Decision* magazine, March 1965, p. 2.
11. Augustine's *Confessions*, Book 6, Chapter 4.
12. 2 Kings 6:6 (KJV).
13. Philippians 1:16.
14. Jude 3.
15. Emile Cailliet, *The Clue to Pascal* (Philadelphia: Westminster Press, 1943), p. 67.
16. Abraham Kuyper, *The Work of the Holy Spirit,* Henri de Vries, trans. (New York: Funk & Wagnalls Co., 1900), pp. 76–78.
17. John 16:8.
18. 2 Timothy 3:16.
19. Isaiah 55:11 (KJV).
20. Acts 8:27-39.
21. Paul B. Smith, *Perilous Times* (London: Marshall, Morgan & Scott, 1967), p. 82.
22. Portions of this chapter appeared in *Decision* magazine, April 1972, p. 2.

Chapter 12. Press-Box Theology

1. G. A. Studdert-Kennedy, "High and Lifted Up," in *The Unutterable Beauty* (London: Hodder & Stoughton, 1947), pp. 47–48.
2. Ray C. Stedman, *Body Life* (Glendale, Calif.: Regal Books, 1972), Chapter 11.
3. See pp. 58–59.
4. Quoted in *Evangelism Alert* (London: World Wide Publications, 1972).
5. *The Living Bible.*
6. John 13:35 (RSV).
7. Luke 3:16 (RSV).
8. Chadwick, *Way to Pentecost,* p. 39.

9. Berle, *Power*, pp. 37, 62.
10. Cf. Luke 10:27.
11. Cf. Galatians 2:20.
12. From my editorial in *Decision* magazine, July 1968, p. 2.

Chapter 13. The Power That Revives

1. Leonard L. Legters, *Victory: The Will of God for Me* (Philadelphia: Christian Life Literature Fund, 1932), pp. 43–44.
2. Cf. Matthew 24:14. See also Joel 2:28-32; Acts 2:17-21.
3. Aldous Huxley, *Time Must Have a Stop* (New York: Harper & Row, 1944), pp. 310–11.
4. Romans 5:20.
5. 2 Chronicles 7:14 (RSV); Joel 2:28 (KJV).
6. Cf. Howard A. Hanke, "Asbury Awakening," *Decision* magazine, May 1970, p. 4.
7. Berle, *Power*, p. 37; see also pp. 59–83.
8. W. W. Sweet, *Revivalism in America* (New York: Charles Scribner's Sons, 1944), p. 181.
9. Quoted *ibid.*, p. 182.
10. See Chapter 12.
11. Genesis 32:25.
12. Cf. John 4:42.
13. John 20:22 (RSV).

Chapter 14. The Church on Fire

1. Billy Graham, "The Spirit of Pentecost," *Decision* magazine, May 1961, pp. 1, 15.
2. See pp. 58–59.
3. John 16:33 (KJV).
4. Isaiah 40:29 (KJV).
5. Frank Houghton, *Amy Carmichael of Dohnavur* (London: S.P.C.K., 1953), p. 284.
6. Matthew 2:10.
7. Hebrews 12:2
8. Acts 8:8.
9. Romans 14:17.

10. Galatians 5:22.
11. 1 John 1:4.
12. A. W. Tozer, *Paths to Power* (Harrisburg, Pa.: Christian Publications, n.d.), p. 36.
13. Galatians 6:1 (KJV).
14. 1 John 3:11 (RSV).
15. Cf. 2 Timothy 1:6.
16. Portions of this chapter appeared in *Decision* magazine, June 1972, p. 2.

Chapter 15. Power Ready and Available

1. This message appeared in one of the last issues of *Spiritual Life,* the magazine founded and edited by Wang Ming-tao in Peking from 1925 to 1955. Sentenced to life imprisonment by the Chinese Communist government for preaching the Gospel, Wang at the time of the present volume's publication was reported alive and still in custody in a "concentration center" in northern Shansi. (Personal note from Leslie T. Lyall, January 31, 1972.)
2. George Whitefield, in John Gillies, *Memoirs of the Rev. George Whitefield* (Hartford: Edwin Hunt & Son, 1853), vol. 2, pp. 609, 613.
3. Hosea 12:3 (KJV).
4. Micah 3:8 (KJV).
5. Psalm 68:35 (KJV).
6. Isaiah 40:29-31 (KJV).
7. Philippians 3:8, 10 (KJV).
8. *Decision* magazine, April 1970, p. 14. (Submitted by John D. McCready, Black Mountain, N. C.)
9. Matthew 11:25.
10. 1 John 4:1 (KJV).
11. 2 Timothy 3:7 (KJV).
12. 2 Corinthians 2:16.
13. Job 1:12 (RSV).
14. Job 13:15 (KJV).
15. Romans 1:26, 28 (KJV).
16. Berle, *Power*, pp. 554–64.
17. "There are other motifs [than reconciliation] which are also soundly

Biblical and contemporaneously relevant. One of these motifs is 're-demption,' the 'liberation' of man through Christ and the Holy Spirit from forces and thralldoms that hold him bound, individually and collectively, and constitute a problem for 'reconciliation' " (John A. Mackay, in *Presbyterian Outlook,* December 13, 1965, p. 5).

18.   1 Corinthians 13:5 (KJV).
19.   Lady Julian of Norwich (1342–1413), *Revelations of Divine Love,* Grace Warrack, ed. (London: Methuen & Co., 1958; first published 1670), pp. 10–11.
20.   Jeremiah 29:13 (RSV).
21.   Psalm 27:8 (KJV).
22.   1 Peter 5:5.

Bibliography

WHILE the literature of the Holy Spirit is vast, surprisingly little appears to have been written on the subject of spiritual power from a Christian point of view, either in ancient or modern times. This bibliography makes no claim to be exhaustive. Some important references not included below will be found in the notes. All the books listed have proved helpful; those marked with a small asterisk are recent writings related to power whose evangelical point of view is congenial to the present volume.

A word should be added about the Scripture translations appearing in these pages. The Authorized Version, the Revised Standard Version, and other modern versions and paraphrases have been drawn upon freely. In each instance the rendering has been sought that would bring into sharpest focus the meaning of the passage quoted. Many times the author has translated directly from the Greek, following the reading in *The Englishman's Greek New Testament* (Grand Rapids, Mich.: Zondervan Publishing Co., 1970 edition).

AUGUSTINE OF HIPPO. *City of God.* Translated by Marcus Dods. Great Books of the Western World (series). Chicago: Encyclopaedia Britannica, 1952.
———. *Confessions.* Translated by Sherwood E. Wirt as *Love Song.* New York: Harper & Row, 1971.
BARTH, KARL. *The Epistle to the Romans.* Translated by Sir Edwyn C. Hoskyns. London: Oxford University Press, 1933.
BERLE, ADOLF A. *Power.* New York: Harcourt Brace Jovanovich, Inc., 1967.
BERNE, ERIC. *Games People Play.* New York: Grove Press, 1964.
BRUNER, FREDERICK DALE. *A Theology of the Holy Spirit.* Grand Rapids, Mich.: William B. Eerdmans Publishing Co., 1970.
*CHADWICK, SAMUEL. *The Way to Pentecost.* London: Hodder & Stoughton, 1932.
*CRISWELL, W. A. *The Holy Spirit in Today's World.* Grand Rapids, Mich.: Zondervan Publishing Co., 1966.

*GESSWEIN, ARMIN. *Is Revival the Normal?* Elizabethtown, Pa.: McBeth Press, 1956.

*GRAHAM, BILLY. *Peace with God.* Garden City, N. Y.: Doubleday & Co., 1953.

*———. *The Jesus Generation.* Grand Rapids, Mich.: Zondervan Publishing Co., 1971.

*GRUBB, NORMAN P. *Rees Howells, Intercessor.* Fort Washington, Pa.: Christian Literature Crusade, 1952.

*HADFIELD, J. A. "The Psychology of Power." In *The Spirit,* edited by B. H. STREETER. London: Macmillan & Co., 1919.

*HESSION, ROY AND REVEL. *The Calvary Road.* Philadelphia: Christian Literature Crusade, 1950.

HOCKING, WILLIAM ERNEST. *Strength of Men and Nations.* New York: Harper & Brothers, 1959.

JULIAN OF NORWICH (LADY JULIAN). *Revelations of Divine Love.* Edited by Grace Warrack. London: Methuen & Co., 1958.

KELLEY, DEAN M. *Why Conservative Churches Are Growing.* New York: Harper & Row, 1972.

KUYPER, ABRAHAM. *The Work of the Holy Spirit.* Translated by Henri de Vries. New York: Funk & Wagnalls Co., 1900.

*LEGTERS, LEONARD L. *The Simplicity of the Spirit-Filled Life.* Farmingdale, N. Y.: Christian Witness Products, 1930.

*———. *Victory: The Will of God for Me.* Philadelphia: Christian Life Literature Fund, 1932.

MACHIAVELLI, NICCOLÒ. *The Prince.* Translated by W. K. Marriott. Great Books of the Western World (series). Chicago: Encyclopaedia Britannica, 1952.

*MCINTIRE, JAMES R. *The Life of the Holy Spirit.* St. Louis, Mo.: Bethany Press, 1930.

*MACKAY, JOHN A. *Christianity on the Frontier.* London: Lutterworth Press, 1950.

*MORGAN, G. CAMPBELL. *The Spirit of God.* New York: Fleming H. Revell Co., 1900.

*MORRIS, LEON. *Spirit of the Living God.* London: Inter-Varsity Press, 1960.

NEWBIGIN, LESSLIE. *The Household of God.* New York: Friendship Press, 1954.

NIEBUHR, REINHOLD. *The Nature and Destiny of Man.* 2 vols. New York: Charles Scribner's Sons, 1941, 1943.

*OLFORD, STEPHEN F. *Heart-Cry for Revival.* New York: Fleming H. Revell Co., 1962.

*OCKENGA, HAROLD J. *Power Through Pentecost.* In *Preaching for Today.* Grand Rapids, Mich.: William B. Eerdmans Publishing Co., 1959.

PASCAL, BLAISE. *The Provincial Letters.* Translated by Thomas McCrie. New York: Modern Library, 1941.

*PAXSON, RUTH. *The Work of God the Holy Spirit.* Chicago: Moody Press, 1958.

*PEDERSON, DUANE C. *The Jesus People.* Glendale, Calif.: Regal Books, 1971.

*PHILLIPS, J. B. *Ring of Truth.* New York: Macmillan & Co., 1967.

*PLOWMAN, EDWARD E. *The Jesus Movement in America.* Elgin, Ill.: David C. Cook Publishing Co., 1971.

POTTER, STEPHEN. *Some Notes on Lifemanship.* London: Rupert Hart-Davis, 1950.

*RAMM, BERNARD. *The Witness of the Spirit.* Grand Rapids, Mich.: William B. Eerdmans Publishing Co., 1959.

*RAVENHILL, LEONARD. *Why Revival Tarries.* Zachary, La.: Fires of Revival, 1959.

REICH, CHARLES A. *The Greening of America.* New York: Random House, 1970.

RUSSELL, BERTRAND. *Power: A New Social Analysis.* New York: W. W. Norton & Co., 1938.

*SANDERS, J. OSWALD. *The Holy Spirit and His Gifts.* Grand Rapids, Mich.: Zondervan Publishing Co., 1970. First published 1940.

*_____. *Spiritual Problems.* Chicago: Moody Press, 1971. First published 1944.

*SHOEMAKER, SAMUEL M. *With the Holy Spirit and with Fire.* New York: Harper & Row, 1960.

*STEDMAN, RAY C. *Body Life.* Glendale, Calif.: Regal Books, 1972.

*STOTT, JOHN R. W. *Basic Christianity.* London: Inter-Varsity Press, 1958.

*_____. *The Baptism and Fullness of the Holy Spirit.* London: Inter-Varsity Press, 1964.

SWEET, W. W. *Revivalism in America.* New York: Charles Scribner's Sons, 1944.

TORREY, REUBEN A. *The Power of Prayer.* Grand Rapids, Mich.: Zondervan Publishing Co., 1971. First published 1924.

*TOZER, A. W. *Paths to Power.* Harrisburg, Pa.: Christian Publications, n.d.

*WALLIS, ARTHUR. *In the Day of Thy Power: The Scriptural Principles of Revival.* London: Christian Literature Crusade, 1956.

WIRT, SHERWOOD E. *Magnificent Promise.* Chicago: Moody Press, 1964.

————. *The Social Conscience of the Evangelical.* New York: Harper & Row, 1968.

Index

Micah, 107
Micaiah, 24
Moody, Dwight L., 36, 92
Morgan, G. Campbell, 45–46, 51, 119–20
Morris, Leon, xv, 40, 48, 119–20
Moses, 24, 27, 44, 99, 103
Munger, Robert Boyd, 85

Nagenda, William, 93
Nature, 4, 11–12, 55
New birth, 43–44, 79, 86, 97–98
Newbigin, Lesslie, 59, 121
Niebuhr, Reinhold, 5, 115
Nietzsche, Friedrich, 2, 115
Niles, D. T., 105
Noah, 12

Occultism, 13, 47, 73
Ockenga, Harold J., 38, 119
Original sin, 4, 8, 75

Pallas Athene, 10
Paraclete, see Holy Spirit
Pascal, Blaise, 25, 58, 77, 117
Patton, General George S., 19–20
Paul, the Apostle, 8–9, 16, 25, 29–31, 36, 38, 43, 55, 58, 62–63, 70, 77–78, 87, 101, 103, 108–109, 111
Peace, 2, 18, 65, 70, 102–103, 111
Peale, Norman Vincent, 61
Pederson, Duane C., 65, 121
Pentecost, 23, 41, 43, 70, 84, 98–99, 107
Peron, Juan, 5
Peter, the Apostle, 31–32, 41, 45, 58
Pharaoh Rameses II, 13
Philip, the Apostle, 101
Phillips, J. B., 74–75, 122
Pike, Christopher, 68
Pike, James, 29, 68
Pilate, Pontius, 42
Plato, 9
Plowman, Edward E., 69, 121
Potter, Stephen, 6, 115
Power, defined, 27; animal, 4; black, 24; Chicano, 24; church, xii, 10, 14, 57; demonic, 12–13, 15, 29; dictatorial, 57; divine, 12, 29, 44, 55, 98; ecclesiastical, 42, 71; hierarchical, 57; human, 1–21, 23–24, 27–29, 31–32, 36, 40, 42, 60, 81, 110, 112; inquisitorial, 57; Jesus, defined, 23; love, see Love; mechanical, 81; military, 57; natural, 23, 28; occult, 13,

Power *cont'd*
47; over environment, 11–13, 15; over self, 14–15; physical, 11, 23; political, 57, 71, 89; psychological, 47; religious, 10, 14, 47; Roman, 45; social, 16, 92; spiritual, ix, xi–xii, 8, 23, 27, 29, 33, 51, 54–55, 71, 77, 83, 92, 98, 101–102; student, 24; supernatural, ix, 22–23, 25, 28, 49, 58, 69, 75, 78, 88, 91, 101, 106, 109; will to power, 2, 5, 11; woman, 24; power drive, 9–10, 13, 15, 17, 21, 78; power failure, xv, 56–57, 62–64; power game, xv, 1–9, 11–12, 17–18, 21, 25, 31, 37, 40, 42–43, 45, 59, 61, 83, 98–99, 110; power of God, xiii, 12–13, 21, 24, 27–32, 37–41, 44, 49, 54–56, 59, 66, 74, 83, 89, 103, 105, 109; power play, 2–3, 9, 40; power structure, 25; power struggle, 6, 8, 10, 14, 19; power vacuum, 34–35, 37–38; powerlessness, 2, 29, 34, 36, 45, 53, 59, 75, 83, 112
Prayer, xii, 37–38, 45, 51–54, 60, 62, 69–71, 82, 90–91, 93, 96
Press-box theology, xi, 81–87
Pride, 1–5, 7–12, 19, 40, 43, 61, 78, 83, 86, 96–97, 109
Psalms, 1
Puritans, 14

Race, racism, 70
Ramm, Bernard, 49, 120
Rapo, 6–7
Ravenhill, Leonard, 94
Reconciliation, 110–11
Redemption, 44, 110–11
Reformation, 90
Reich, Charles A., 10, 116
Repentance, 58, 78, 97
Rest, 104, 111; and power, 102–103
Resurrection, 28, 36, 107
Revival, ix, xi–xii, 33, 45, 67, 69, 71, 88–99, 101–102, 104, 112; defined, 92; at Asbury College, xi, 90–91; in Canada, xii, 94, 96 (Regina, 94, 104; Saskatoon, 94, 104; Winnipeg, 94–95, 104, 112); in East Africa, 93, 99; in Kentucky, 69; at Mount Hermon, 93; on the Outer Hebrides (Scotland), 67; in South Africa, 104; in Wales, 101–102
Richard III, 5
Richelieu, Cardinal, 20
Roman Catholicism, 14, 70

72 73 74 75 10 9 8 7 6 5 4 3 2 1